Prevention
and Intervention Practice
in Post-Apartheid South Africa

Prevention and Intervention Practice in Post-Apartheid South Africa has been co-published simultaneously as *Journal of Prevention & Intervention in the Community*, Volume 25, Number 1 2003.

Prevention and Intervention Practice in Post-Apartheid South Africa

Vijé Franchi, PhD
Editor

Norman Duncan, PhD
Consulting Editor

Prevention and Intervention Practice in Post-Apartheid South Africa has been co-published simultaneously as *Journal of Prevention & Intervention in the Community*, Volume 25, Number 1 2003.

Routledge
Taylor & Francis Group

NEW YORK AND LONDON

Prevention and Intervention Practice in Post-Apartheid South Africa has been co-published simultaneously as *Journal of Prevention & Intervention in the Community*™, Volume 25, Number 1 2003.

First published 2003 by The Haworth Press, Inc.

Published 2024
by Routledge
605 Third Avenue, New York, NY 10158

and by Routledge
4 Park Square, Milton Park, Abingdon, Oxon OX14 4RN

Routledge is an imprint of the Taylor & Francis Group, an informa business

Library of Congress Cataloging-in-Publication Data

Prevention and intervention practice in post-apartheid South Africa / Vijé Franchi, Norman Duncan, editors.
      p. cm.
      "Has been co-published simultaneously as Journal of prevention & intervention in the community, volume 25, number 1, 2003."
      Includes bibliographical references and index.
      ISBN 0-7890-2104-8 (hardcover : alk paper) – ISBN 0-7890-2105-6 (softcover : alk. paper)
      1. Violence–South Africa–Prevention. 2. Political violence–South Africa–Prevention. 3. Political participation–South Africa. 4. Community leadership–South Africa. 5. South Africa–Politics and government–1994- 6. South Africa–Social conditions–1994- 7. South Africa–Race relations. I. Franchi, Vijé. II. Duncan, Norman, PhD. III. Journal of prevention & intervention in the community.
HN801.Z9V5683 2003
303.6'0968–dc21

                                                                                    2003005363

Cover design by Lora Wiggins

ISBN: 978-0-7890-2104-5 (hbk)
ISBN: 978-0-7890-2105-2 (pbk)
ISBN: 978-1-315-78578-3 (ebk)

DOI: 10.4324/9781315785783

ABOUT THE EDITOR

Vijé Franchi, PhD, is Associate Professor/Senior Lecturer at the Institute of Psychology, Lyon II University in Lyon, France, where she has developed and integrated modules of teaching theoretical and methodological approaches to intercultural and community training, research, and evaluation. She is a clinical and community psychologist who has played an active role in developing community prevention and research projects in South Africa and France. She is a member of the Institute for Policy Studies in Education (IPSE) Research unit at the University of Paris X in Nanterre, France, and is one of the founding members of the Group for the Study of Asymmetrical Relations.

In 2001, Dr. Franchi was invited to participate in the development of an International Research Unit on the Study of Racism and Related Phenomena and the following year, was commissioned to write the European Information Network of Racism and Xenophobia (RAXEN) analytic report on discrimination in education in France. She edited a special issue of the *International Journal of Intercultural Relations* that dealt with current perspectives of race, racism, and intercultural relations in post-apartheid South Africa.

ABOUT THE CONSULTING EDITOR

Norman Duncan, PhD, holds the position of Associate Professor at the Institute for Social and Health Sciences at the University of South Africa. He previously served as Chair of the Department of Psychology at the University of the Western Cape and subsequently as Head of the Department of Psychology at the University of Venda. He is currently the Editor of the *South African Journal of Psychology* and one of the two Editors-in-Chief of *African Safety Promotion: A Journal of Injury and Violence Prevention*.

Prevention
and Intervention Practice
in Post-Apartheid South Africa

CONTENTS

Preface   xv

Introduction   1
    Vijé Franchi
    Norman Duncan

Promoting Methodological Pluralism, Theoretical Diversity
    and Interdisciplinarity Through a Multi-Leveled
    Violence Prevention Initiative in South Africa   11
    Garth Stevens
    Mohamed Seedat
    Tanya M. Swart
    Clinton van der Walt

The Use of Public Health Research in Stimulating Violence
    and Injury Prevention Practices and Policies:
    Reflections from South Africa   31
    Mohamed Seedat
    Anabela Nascimento

Women's Leadership Programs in South Africa: A Strategy
    for Community Intervention   49
    Cheryl de la Rey
    Gia Jankelowitz
    Shahaaz Suffla

Intervening in Communities at Multiple Levels:
    Combining Curative and Preventive Interventions   65
    Anthony V. Naidoo
    Sherine Van Wyk

Building Health Promoting and Inclusive Schools
in South Africa: Community-Based Prevention in Action   81
   Bridget Johnson
   Sandy Lazarus

Rapid Assessment Procedures: A Participatory Action Research
Approach to Field Training in Community Prevention
and Intervention   99
   Vijé Franchi
   Tanya M. Swart

Index   117

Preface

Like many other African and 'developing' countries, South Africa is currently faced with a myriad of social problems and challenges, including rapidly escalating levels of poverty and childhood malnutrition; intolerably high rates of crime and violence, particularly against women and children; inordinately high levels of substance abuse; and a disquietingly rapid surge in HIV/AIDS infection rates. Of all these problems, the HIV/AIDS infection rates appear to be the most daunting. Recent research indicates that approximately one-fifth of South Africa's population between 15 and 49 years of age are infected with the human-immunodeficiency virus. Furthermore, it is predicted that by the year 2010 the average life expectancy for South Africans will have dropped from the current 68.2 years to 48 years.[1] The expected consequences of these infections and life expectancy rates include sharply escalating levels of poverty, a significant upsurge in the number of orphans and child-headed families, and growing numbers of desperate, destitute children drawn into cycles of crime and prostitution in their attempts to escape the starvation and want that will inevitably face them.[2]

It is against the backdrop of this virulent web of unfolding social problems, as well as their potentially debilitating impact on the psychosocial well-being of South African communities that the contributors to this volume attempt to engage with the subject matter and key concerns of community psychology; and it is herein, in fact, that lies the true allure and value of this concise, yet thoroughly challenging volume. To its credit, this volume addresses some of the key theoretical positions and debates in contemporary community psychology, not *in abstracto*, as so many psychology volumes tend to do, but by means of an appurte-

---

[Haworth co-indexing entry note]: "Preface." Norman Duncan. Co-published simultaneously in *Journal of Prevention & Intervention in the Community* (The Haworth Press, Inc.) Vol. 25, No. 1, 2003, pp. xvii-xviii; and: *Prevention and Intervention Practice in Post-Apartheid South Africa* (ed: Vijé Franchi; cons. ed: Norman Duncan) The Haworth Press, Inc., 2003, pp. xv-xvi.

nant scrutiny of the real problems currently faced by real communities in South Africa. It is largely because of this synergistic approach that the volume is able to captivate from beginning to end.

However, this volume does not merely concern itself with explicating and illustrating the key positions and debates in community psychology; it also challenges the reader to critically engage with some of the many complex social problems endemic to countries such as South Africa, as well as the capacity of community psychology, as discipline and practice, to effectively deal with these problems. As reflected in its title, the pursuit of best practices in community prevention and intervention is central to this volume.

In a sense, the volume, both through what it is able to articulate, as well as what it does not, or is unable to articulate, represents a challenge to community psychology to constantly re-evaluate and re-invent its theory, methods and practices, so that it can more effectively contribute to the well-being of communities, particularly marginalized, under-resourced and disempowered communities.

The authors of the chapters contained in this volume, namely, Cheryl de la Rey, Vijé Franchi, Gia Jankelowitz, Shahaaz Suffla, Bridget Johnson, Sandy Lazarus, Anthony Naidoo, Anabela Nascimento, Clinton van der Walt, Shirene Van Wyk, Tanya Swart, Mohamed Seedat, and Garth Stevens, should all be commended, not only for their keen analyses of the many difficulties currently confronting many South African communities, but also for their attempts, by way of their contributions to this volume, to help develop and shape a community psychology that will make a difference in South Africa as well as in other similar contexts.

This volume, *Prevention and Intervention Practice in Post-Apartheid South Africa,* makes for truly captivating reading.

Norman Duncan
Institute for Social and Health Sciences
University of South Africa

NOTES

1. Dorrington, R., Bourne, D., Bradshaw, D., Laubscher, R. & Timaeus, I. (2001). *The impact of HIV/AIDS on adult mortality in South Africa.* Tygerberg: South African Medical Research Council.

2. Fourie, P. & SchontNich, M. (2001). Africa's new security threat. HIV/AIDS and human security in Southern Africa. *African Security Review, 10*(4), <*http://www. iss.co.za.Pubs/ASR/10No4Fourie.html*>. Accessed on October 7, 2002.

Introduction

Vijé Franchi

Institute of Psychology, University of Lyon 2

Norman Duncan

Institute of Social and Health Sciences, University of South Africa

In 1985, Dawes argued that apartheid policies engineered a set of socio-economic conditions that were extremely hostile to the psychosocial well-being of the majority of South Africans. These conditions included extreme levels of poverty, untenable levels of interpersonal violence and crime, and deplorably high rates of ill-health, with black and lower-income communities most adversely affected (Butchart & Seedat, 1990; Dawes, 1985; Foster & Swartz, 1997).

Today, several years after the collapse of apartheid as a political system, research reveals that many of these conditions continue to exert their pernicious influence on South African society. Indeed, a number of recent publications report the widening and crippling grip of poverty (Robinson & Biersteker, 1997; May, 1998; Van Niekerk, 2002), the growing prevalence of crime and violence (Burrows, Bowman, Matzopoulos &

We wish to acknowledge the following reviewers for their incisive and valuable contribution: K. Gibson (University of Cape Town), G. Horenczyk (Hebrew University of Jerusalem), I. Ricardo (George Washington University, Washington, DC), M.J. Terre Blanche (University of South Africa), A. Van Niekerk (Medical and Research Council).

[Haworth co-indexing entry note]: "Introduction." Franchi, Vijé, and Norman Duncan. Co-published simultaneously in *Journal of Prevention & Intervention in the Community* (The Haworth Press, Inc.) Vol. 25, No. 1, 2003, pp. 1-9; and: *Prevention and Intervention Practice in Post-Apartheid South Africa* (ed: Vijé Franchi; cons. ed: Norman Duncan) The Haworth Press, Inc., 2003, pp. 1-9.

Van Niekerk, 2001), and the disquietingly rapid surge in the HIV/AIDS infection rates in South Africa (Dorrington, Bourne, Bradshaw et al., 2001; Love Life, 2002).

According to Van Niekerk (2002), between 40 and 50 percent of the South African population are currently living in abject poverty. Furthermore, Robinson & Biersteker (1997) report that 60 percent of this grouping of South Africans are under the age of 18 years, i.e., children. Additionally, recent surveys indicate that 68 percent of South African mothers tested HIV-positive in 1999 (Dorrington, Bourne, Bradshaw et al., 2001); and that approximately 26% of women and 12% of men aged between 20 and 24 were infected with HIV (Love Life, 2002). This gloomy picture is darkened even further by the ever-present specter of violence. In 1996, Butchart, Nell and Seedat found that the incidence rate for violent death was amongst the highest in the world. This finding was confirmed by a recent study conducted by Burrows, Bowman, Matzopoulos and Van Niekerk (2001). This latter study found that homicide currently constitutes the single major cause of fatalities amongst male adolescents in South Africa. Amongst females, external injuries are prominent, but less so than is the case with males. However, both males and females have a very high exposure to crime, especially, violent crime (Burrows, Bowman, Matzopoulos and Van Niekerk, 2001). Here it should be noted that the persistence and proliferation of these problems are not simply a result of the inability of the present South African government to deal with the legacy of apartheid. Rather, as is the case in most other lower-income countries, these problems are largely also the result of the unbridled greed of powerful countries and the conditions of globalization, which are steadily exacerbating the problems faced by lower-income countries so as to secure ever-increasing benefits for 'developed' countries (Blustein, 2002; Bond, 2000; Reynolds, 1997. Also see Seedat & Nascimento in this volume).

All the above-mentioned problems obviously have the potential to profoundly undermine the psychosocial well-being of South African communities, particularly black, lower-income and rural communities, and the aged, women and children within these communities who, according to all indications, are most vulnerable to these problems (May, 1998; Van Niekerk, 2002).

There can be no denying that, along with the other health sciences and professions, community psychology in South Africa, potentially, can play an important role in addressing these problems. However, as previously argued (see Seedat, Duncan & Lazarus, 2001), if it wishes to play a meaningful role in addressing the problems faced by contemporary

South Africa; if indeed, it wishes to play any role in the transformation of South African society , it will be imperative for community psychology in this country to endeavor: (1) to extend mental health service provision to all citizens, particularly historically oppressed, marginalized or disadvantaged communities; (2) to challenge and reconstruct or transform existing conceptualizations of the causes and development of extant psychosocial problems; (3) to afford due consideration to contextual factors when addressing these problems; (4) to challenge traditional paradigms within which psychology operates, by prioritizing prevention over curative interventions; and (5) to broaden the role definition and scope of intervention of psychologists responding to prevailing psychosocial problems and the conditions giving rise to these problems (Seedat et al., 2001).

In their review of the development of community psychology as academic discipline and mental health intervention system, Seedat et al. (2001) conclude that despite its attempts to adhere to objectives such as those listed above, and despite its "indisputable accomplishments," community psychology in South Africa unfortunately still has to achieve what Gordon and Shipman (1988) refer to as "distributive equality" and "distributive sufficiency" (p. 5). Very simply put, distributive equality refers to political representation and social justice. Distributive sufficiency, on the other hand refers to the capacity to promote the well-being of under-resourced, historically marginalized and oppressed communities through the transformation of the socio-political and economic conditions that compromise the psychosocial well-being of these groups.

In our opinion, distributive sufficiency can be attained most effectively and enduringly through interventions that are underpinned by what Rappaport (1981, p. 15) refers to as "the logic of empowerment." Despite the manner in which the concept, "empowerment," has been distorted over the years (Rissel, 1994) and despite the caution that writers such as Orford (1992) and Rissel (1994) sound in relation to the use of the concept, we find the principles and values underlying the concept – particularly as articulated by Rappaport (1981) – of abiding critical value to community psychology and its attempts to contribute to social transformation, particularly within the South African context.

At the risk of over-simplifying a fairly complex construct, empowerment can briefly be defined as a process by means of which people and groups gain control over their lives through claiming and exercising their democratic right to participate in, or challenge the social, political and economic institutions that structure their lived reality (Rappaport,

1984; Rissel, 1994). According to Rappaport (1981), empowerment should constitute one of the key reference points of interventions aimed at enhancing communities' well-being–particularly in the case of socially and economically marginalized communities; for it is only when community empowerment becomes an integral aspect of community interventions that the impact of these interventions will be maximally effective and lasting.

In his seminal, and by now classic work, *In praise of paradox: A social policy of empowerment over prevention,* Rappaport (1981) argues that community psychologists could play a significant role in facilitating the empowerment of communities. However, according to him, in order for them to be maximally effective in this regard, community psychologists should strive to meet several basic requirements, three of which are presented here. Firstly, it is incumbent upon community psychologists to identify and examine the ways in which communities may already be attempting to deal with impediments to their well-being and functioning. Secondly, it is essential that community psychologists uncover and critically examine the social structures and conditions within which people's problems of living develop. Thirdly, it is imperative that community psychologists remain open to learning from the ways in which communities attempt to solve their problems. If the strategies communities employ to solve their problems prove to be effective, then the community psychologist should make these more public, so as to validate and valorize local knowledges and solutions. This is intended to contribute to the development of appropriate interventions that will "make it more, rather than less likely that [those] not now handling their own problems in living or [who are] shut out from current solutions, gain control over their lives" (Rappaport, 1981, p. 15).

The above-mentioned imperatives underline three important axioms central to progressive community psychology theory and practice. Firstly, when communities experience difficulties in living or functioning optimally, considering the contexts within which these difficulties occur is crucial to understanding the genesis of, and facilitating solutions to these difficulties. While it has long been accepted by psychologists that communities' problems are invariably a consequence of the interaction between individual and environmental factors, the 'helping' professions have traditionally tended to focus only on the "person" side of the equation–at the expense of the social structures and processes implicated in these problems (Orford, 1992). This orientation inevitably results in the generation of solutions that attempt to teach individuals to 'fit into' deficient social institutions and processes, instead of solutions that attempt to transform these institutions and processes so that they more adequately meet the needs of communities (Rappaport, 1981).

Secondly, people are capable of, and have the right to participate in solving the social problems that impede the achievement of their well-being. One of the key reasons accounting for why many communities experience difficulties in living is because they have been deprived of the right to participate fully in the processes and institutions that structure their lives. Attempting to do things on behalf of communities, as the 'helping' professions have tended to do for so many years, simply serves to exacerbate their loss of control over their own lives, and in the process aggravates their problems in living.

Thirdly, because they are largely structured by the confluence of fairly specific or localized conditions and factors, the difficulties in living or optimal functioning faced by every community are unique, and as such, require unique, locally appropriate–rather than universal or generalizable–solutions. As Rappaport (1981) cautions, community psychology should avoid the tendency of so many 'helping' professions to search for universal or monolithic solutions. Not only does this tendency lead to the development of psychosocial interventions that are inappropriate for many communities, but it also sets up the community psychologist as *the* expert, and the recipients of her or his *expertise* as incapable of playing a meaningful role in solving their problems of living.

This volume, *Prevention and Intervention Practice in Post-Apartheid South Africa*, focuses on the attempts of a small group of psychologists to critically search for, and examine, appropriate frameworks for community-based and directed praxis that provide locally constructed, contextually appropriate responses to some of the most pressing problems confronting post-apartheid South Africa; responses that have the potential to engender community empowerment and distributive sufficiency as conceptualized by Rappaport (1981) and Gordon and Shipman (1988), respectively.

To a certain extent, the six chapters included in this volume represent a sample of the range and variety of conceptual frameworks and intervention practices developed by South African community psychology in its attempts to contribute more contextually relevant and community-empowering responses to the challenges that confront present-day South African society. While quite diverse in orientation and focus, these chapters are all linked together by their manifest commitment to community empowerment and to meeting the prerequisites that Rappaport (1981) has identified for effectively achieving this goal. We now turn to a brief summary of the content of these chapters.

The first chapter by Stevens, Seedat, Swart, and van der Walt examines the conceptual basis for synthesizing relevant aspects of the public health approach with a community development approach to violence prevention interventions and research in South Africa. Furthermore, the chapter examines the manner in which this synthesis of approaches would facilitate "interdisciplinarity, methodological pluralism, theoretical diversity and community empowerment." Partly by way of illustrating this scrutiny, the chapter considers the preliminary outcomes of a pilot implementation of a multi-level violence prevention matrix developed in a low-income neighborhood in South Africa by a local research institute, and which draws on both the public health and community development approaches. The chapter also includes an incisive and highly informative evaluation of these approaches to violence prevention.

The second chapter by Seedat and Nascimento explores the utility of epidemiological data in attempts to inform injury and violence prevention interventions. In addition, the chapter examines the factors that influence the use of epidemiological data in policy formulation and interventions in respect of violence prevention. One of the key strengths of this chapter lies in its pointed focus on the importance of citizen participation in the use of epidemiological data to inform policies and interventions aimed at reducing injuries within communities. Furthermore, the chapter presents a strong case for the generation of "local research data" to develop interventions that are appropriate for local contexts (cf. Rappaport, 1981).

Addressing gender development in general, and its role in empowering communities in specific, the next chapter by de la Rey, Jankelowitz and Suffla reviews women's leadership training programs in South Africa in a critical search for best practices. A key assumption informing this chapter is that the empowerment and training of women for leadership roles is central to the empowerment and development of communities as a whole (cf. Orford, 1992). Indeed, this was the point of departure for the study on which this chapter is based. The study revealed several important findings that may have important implications for the development of appropriate interventions aimed at leadership development, the capacitation of women, as well as community empowerment and development in South Africa and elsewhere.

In the fourth chapter in this volume, Naidoo and Van Wyk propose a multi-focused intervention strategy as a possible means of responding to some of the socio-psychological sequelae of the profound socio-economic inequalities still confronting post-apartheid South African society. Using the implementation of this intervention strategy in Jamestown, a peri-urban community in the Western Cape region of South Africa as exemplar, Naidoo and Van Wyk explore and persuasively articulate the importance of community partnerships and empowerment as a possible means of promoting equal access to mental health resources so as to start addressing some of the more vexing problems confronting particularly young people in post-1994 South Africa. In addition, the chapter provides a keen examination of what it refers to as "the politics of problem definition" and the asymmetrical relations of power existing between community psychologists as practitioners and researchers, on the one hand, and the communities that they endeavor to serve, on the other.

In the next chapter, Johnson and Lazarus focus on school communities as possible contexts for community-based interventions aimed at dealing with some of the problems that place young people at risk, problems such as violence, poverty, and HIV/AIDS. Furthermore, using the fairly innovative practices employed in a school in a disadvantaged community close to Cape Town as illustration, the chapter explores the potential of the health promoting and inclusive schools approaches in facilitating the development and implementation of holistic strategies to address these and other problems faced by young people–and particularly young people from disadvantaged backgrounds–within the education system. Ultimately, this chapter represents a very persuasive argument for the utility of schools as contexts for, and vehicles of community empowerment and consequently, social transformation.

The role of schools in promoting health and addressing risk factors such as poverty, HIV/AIDS, violence, learning difficulties, substance abuse and delinquency, is a theme that is also taken up–albeit indirectly– in the Franchi and Swart chapter. In their chapter though, Franchi and Swart also focus on deracializing psychological services and practice. Given South Africa's highly racialised and racist past, and given the paucity of literature on the impact of this past on service provision in the health sector, this focus is most appurtenant. Very importantly too, the chapter forcefully argues for the need for, and the utility of accessing communities' understandings of the nature, origins and solutions to the problems impeding their development and well-being.

Collectively, these chapters open a window onto, not only many of the problems that are endemic to the communities constructed through the historically orchestrated violence of apartheid, but also some of the ways in which South African community psychology is, and should be, responding to these problems. Consistent with the views of Rappaport (1981) and Rissel (1994), all these chapters stress the importance of community empowerment as an integral aspect of better practices in preventative and other intervention strategies aimed at dealing with some of the problems facing South African communities.

Furthermore, the detailed presentation and critical analysis of community intervention practices (in the quest for better practices) contained in these chapters provide a lens through which the reader is encouraged to critically engage with the many complex questions related to the relevance and distributive sufficiency of community psychology theory, method and practice, not only in South Africa, but also in other contexts.

Importantly, this collection of chapters also points to various challenges facing community psychology in South Africa and elsewhere: challenges such as developing strategies to enhance the appropriate use of research data in policy formulation; funding constraints which hamper the development, implementation and evaluation of appropriate interventions to deal with marginalized communities' problems; developing appropriate strategies to enhance community empowerment; the on-going difficulties faced by mental health workers due to the racialised divisions inscribed in South African society as a result of past apartheid policies; and the ever-widening gap between poor and wealthy communities. It is obviously only through engaging with these and the many other challenges facing it that community psychology in South Africa will be able to make a meaningful contribution to dealing with the myriad of obstacles to psychosocial well-being currently facing the majority of South Africans, including those identified at the beginning of this chapter. To a certain extent, this volume represents an attempt to contribute to these endeavors.

REFERENCES

Blustein, P. (2002, October 1). Making sense of the impossible. *The Star*, p. 13.

Bond, P. (2000). *Elite transition*. London: Pluto Press.

Burrows, S., Bowman, B., Matzopoulos, R. & Van Niekerk, A. (2001). *A profile of fatal inuries in South Africa 2000; Second Annual Report of the National Injury Mortality Surveillance System.* Tygerberg: Medical Research Council.

Butchart, A., Neil, V. & Seedat, M. (1996). Violence in South Africa: Its definition and prevention as a public health problem. Paper prepared for inclusion in Seager, J. & Parry, C. (Eds.), *Urbanisation and Health In South Africa*. Tygerberg: Medical Research Council.

Butchart, A. & Seedat, M. (1996). Within and without: Images of community and implications for South African psychology. *Social Science Medicine, 31*(10), 1093-1102.

Dawes, A. (1985). Politics and mental health: The position of clinical psychology in South Africa. *South African Journal of Psychology, 15*, 55-61.

Dorrington, R., Bourne, D., Bradshaw, D., Laubscher, R. & Timaeus, I.M. (2001). *The impact of HIV/AIDS on adult mortality in South Africa. Technical Report: Burden of Disease Research Unit.* Tygerberg: Medical Research Council.

Foster, D. & Swartz, S. (1997). Introduction: Policy considerations. In D. Foster, M. Freeman & Y. Pillay (Eds.), *Mental health policy issues for South Africa* (pp. 1-22). Pinelands: MASA Media Publications.

Gordon, E.W. & Shipman, S. (1988). Human diversity and pedagogy. In E.W. Gordon and Associates (Eds.), *Human diversity and pedagogy.* New Haven: Yale University.

Human Rights Watch (2002). *<http://www.ippf.org/resource/gbv/chogm99/foster.htm>* 1 June 2002.

Love Life (2002). *<http://www.lovelife.org.za>* 1 June 2002.

May, J. (1998). *Poverty and inequality in South Africa.* Report prepared for the office of the Executive Deputy President and the Inter-Ministerial Committee for Poverty and Inequality. *<http://www.polity.org.za/govdocs/reports/poverty.html>* 23 September 2002.

Orford, J. (1992). *Community psychology: Theory and practice.* Chichester: Wiley.

Rappaport, J. (1981). In praise of paradox: A social policy of empowerment over prevention. *American Journal of Community Psychology, 9*(1), 1- 21.

Reynolds, P. (1997). Vision: Well being and suffering. In D. Foster, M. Freeman & Y. Pillay (Eds.), *Mental health policy issues for South Africa* (pp. 23 -31). Pinelands: MASA Media Publications.

Rissel, C. (1994). Empowerment: The holy grail of health promotion? *Health Promotion International, 9*(1), 39-45.

Robinson, S. & Biersteker, L. (1997). *The first call; the South African children's budget.* IDASA: Cape Town.

Seedat, M., Duncan, N., & Lazarus, S. (2001). Community psychology: Theory, method, and practice. In M. Seedat, N. Duncan & S. Lazarus (Eds.), *Community Psychology. Theory, Method and Practice* (pp. 3-14). Cape Town: Oxford University Press.

Van Niekerk, A. (2002). *Burn injuries in early childhood: Studies on household, familial and developmental risk factors.* Unpublished Doctoral Research proposal. Karolinska Institutet, Stockholm.

Promoting Methodological Pluralism, Theoretical Diversity and Interdisciplinarity Through a Multi-Leveled Violence Prevention Initiative in South Africa

Garth Stevens
Mohamed Seedat
Tanya M. Swart
Clinton van der Walt

University of South Africa

SUMMARY. Violence prevention within low-income, under-resourced communities presents significant challenges to community development researcher-practitioners seeking to maximize partnerships, resource uti-

Garth Stevens is a clinical psychologist and researcher-practitioner with interests in critical social psychological approaches to understanding violence, racism and forms of inequality and difference, but with an emphasis on models of prevention and intervention that are directly pertinent to these social phenomena.

Mohamed Seedat (D. Phil.) is a clinical psychologist, and is currently professor and director of the Institute for Social and Health Sciences at the University of South Africa.

Tanya M. Swart and Clinton van der Walt are community-counseling psychologists.

Address correspondence to: Garth Stevens, Institute for Social and Health Sciences, University of South Africa, P.O. Box 1087, Lenasia, 1820, South Africa (E-mail: steveg@unisa.ac.za) (G. Stevens).

Acknowledgments and thanks are extended to all staff of the MRC-UNISA Crime, Violence and Injury Lead Program whose joint efforts are reflected in this article.

[Haworth co-indexing entry note]: "Promoting Methodological Pluralism, Theoretical Diversity and Interdisciplinarity Through a Multi-Leveled Violence Prevention Initiative in South Africa." Stevens, Garth et al. Co-published simultaneously in *Journal of Prevention & Intervention in the Community* (The Haworth Press, Inc.) Vol. 25, No. 1, 2003, pp. 11-29; and: *Prevention and Intervention Practice in Post-Apartheid South Africa* (ed: Vijé Franchi; cons. ed: Norman Duncan) The Haworth Press, Inc., 2003, pp. 11-29.

lization and overall program effectiveness. This article highlights a South African research and service delivery organization's efforts to develop a violence prevention matrix, premised upon an adaptation of the public health approach and the infusion of a critical, community development praxis. It presents preliminary outcomes of a multi-level pilot application of this matrix in a low-income neighborhood in South Africa, specifically focusing on evaluating its capacity to foster methodological pluralism, theoretical diversity and interdisciplinarity, together with promoting community empowerment and coalition-building strategies. *[Article copies available for a fee from The Haworth Document Delivery Service: 1-800-HAWORTH. E-mail address: <docdelivery@haworthpress.com> Website: <http://www.HaworthPress.com> © 2003 by The Haworth Press, Inc. All rights reserved.]*

KEYWORDS. Violence prevention, public health, community empowerment, coalition building, South Africa

INTRODUCTION

Violence and its prevention have been central to the history of the South African social formation and a crucial focus of social inquiry for several decades. Prior to 1994, many forms of violence were understood by many primarily as a consequence of the socio-structural processes of apartheid policy that had generated a cyclical and self-perpetuating culture of violence (Dawes, 1990; Duncan & Rock, 1994; Straker, 1992). Others approached this phenomenon from a criminal justice-perspective, and focused on deterrence (e.g., more visible policing) and incapacitation (e.g., harsher bail conditions, punishment and incarceration), rather than socio-political transformation (Butchart, 1996; Schonteich, 1999). In the years post-1994, the holistic prevention, reduction and control of violence emerged as a public health issue (Butchart, Nell & Seedat, 1996; Seedat, 1995; Emmett & Butchart, 2000). More recently, Butchart and Kruger (2001) have argued for the fusion of public health and community psychology approaches to violence prevention. Whilst they all contribute to epistemological, ontological, methodological and theoretical pluralism within contemporary violence prevention endeavors in South Africa, the lack of an overt and structured interface between these varied perspectives tends to increase the potential fragmentation of the violence prevention sector.

This article attempts to expand on the work of Butchart and Kruger (2001), amongst others, by suggesting ways in which public health and community development approaches can be integrated to allow for methodological pluralism, theoretical diversity and interdisciplinarity in the process of community empowerment, sectoral and intersectoral coalition-building. It reflects on a multi-leveled, evidence-led violence prevention initiative in a low-income South African community and reports on some of the potential benefits and challenges emerging from this approach.

CHALLENGES FOR VIOLENCE PREVENTION IN SOUTH AFRICA

Recent national studies indicate that homicides accounted for the largest proportion (45%) of all fatal injuries during 2000, with firearms being the primary external cause of death. This staggering statistic provides some insight into the nature, magnitude and consequences of violence in South Africa, especially considering that those most affected are aged between 15 and 45 years (Burrows, Bowman, Matzopoulos & van Niekerk, 2001). However, more complex understandings of its determinants, antecedents and triggers are required, as interventions directed at this socially and historically embedded phenomenon are more likely to be successful if they are comprehensive, multi-level and guided by theoretical and trans-disciplinary diversity.

Associated with this challenge to community violence prevention is the current status of related service delivery. Since the early 1990s South African society has seen processes of rapid transformation in the political, social and economic realms, which have had significant effects on approaches to service delivery in the health, welfare, education and criminal justice sectors. Whilst significant policy shifts were introduced to redress apartheid disparities in service delivery, strict fiscal discipline during the transformation process placed budgetary constraints on 'welfarist' spending in contemporary South Africa (Bond, 1994, 2000; Werner & Sanders, 1997). These macro-shifts have also raised a new set of challenges within organizations representative of civil society. Prior to 1994, non-governmental organizations (NGOs) acted as social organs that were primarily directed towards the fundamental democratization and political transformation of the apartheid state. In the period following 1994, NGOs increasingly became organs of a normalized civil society and were expected to monitor and affect changes; assist government in service delivery; and secure their own funding. Despite compelling many NGOs to sharpen their programmatic foci, management and strategic visioning, these contextual changes have impacted negatively on the responsiveness and capacity of civil society and the public sector to creatively address community-based violence prevention (Fitzgerald, 1995).

Notwithstanding the existence of a diverse range of projects at present (e.g., conflict resolution and mediation, peace promotion, cross-cultural dialoguing and communication, victim empowerment, health and safety promotion, crisis intervention for trauma victims and primary health care), the violence prevention sector in South Africa remains fairly uncoordinated, with programmatic redundancy and resource wastage. In addition, despite the proliferation of programs, few evaluations regarding their impact have been generated to plan for comprehensive, co-ordinated, cost-effective, sustainable and replicable interventions (Stevens, 2000). The sector remains fragmented, territorial, and too often discipline specific, thereby compromising holistic interventions.

Furthermore, interventions within this sector have often been targeted either at the macro- (e.g., policy changes) or micro- (e.g., individual or small group interventions) levels. Both of these tend to assume a diffusion of their impact, with policy changes and individual changes at some point 'trickling down' to the community level and translating into development. However, interventions do not always contribute to the development of a critical mass of skills, resources, empowerment, self-reliance, trust and cohesion in communities ravaged by violence. Rather, they facilitate the development of individual 'human capital,' and often at the expense of 'social capital.'[1]

Despite the growing recognition of the need for primary research in the violence prevention sector, there is a paucity of reliable, quality information that can drive interventions, policies and evaluations (Burrows, 2000). Whilst research continues at private levels, no comprehensive database on national health information currently exists in South Africa. Existing health and criminal justice statistics also appear to be rudimentary and primarily descriptive in nature.

An additional challenge involves overcoming the binary that arbitrarily separates research and service delivery. Research has historically been constructed as the domain of academics at higher learning institutions, with many community activists viewing research as decontextualised and detached from 'real' community work, thereby further complicating co-alition-building and participatory endeavors (Pretorius-Heuchert & Ahmed, 2001).

A reciprocally dismissive view was often held by academics and researchers toward community activists in NGOs. NGOs were often viewed as operating on political rhetoric without adequately evaluating their practices. This served in part to hamper the documentation of successful grassroots efforts. What belied this seemingly circular debate were the central issues of knowledge production and power. Those involved in academic institutions placed greater value on knowledge derived from traditional social scientific argument, whilst community practitioners were more invested in validating and eliciting organic forms of knowledge (Ahmed & Pretorius-Heuchert, 2001). However, with the contextual shifts within South Africa, researchers are increasingly being pressured to indicate the applied social value of their research, in order to maintain grants and tenure. Similarly, NGOs are faced with increasing demands to facilitate state support for their programs, to influence policy and the legislature, and to generate cost-effective, sustainable, soundly evaluated interventions.

With a new layer of academics, practitioners, researchers and community activists recognizing the need to seek a synergy between research and service delivery, epistemological, ontological and methodological tensions have also arisen around what constitutes good scientific practice (Ahmed & Pretorius-Heuchert, 2001; Bhana & Kanjee, 2001). This often translates into debates about the value of more participatory and qualitative research (e.g., illuminative evaluation) versus more quantitative research (e.g., randomized control trials) as the pinnacle of good scientific evidence, which undermines methodological pluralism, or "methodological eclecticism" (Bhana & Kanjee, 2001), and acts as an additional obstacle to addressing violence in a comprehensive manner.

PUBLIC HEALTH AND COMMUNITY DEVELOPMENT: TOWARDS AN INTEGRATED APPROACH TO VIOLENCE PREVENTION IN COMMUNITIES

The increased utilization of the public health approach in violence prevention (World Health Organization [WHO], 2001), and its adaptation for use within South African communities has been well documented (see, for example, Butchart, 1996; Butchart & Kruger, 2001; Seedat, 1995; Emmett & Butchart, 2000). The present article focuses more specifically on the conceptual basis for merging aspects of public health with a community development approach, and the manner in which this facilitates interdisciplinarity, methodological pluralism, theoretical diversity, community empowerment, as well as sectoral and intersectoral coalition-building.

As separate frameworks for research and intervention in the area of violence prevention, public health and community development approaches are driven by differing epistemologies, ontologies, methodologies and theoretical understandings. Given that the public health model was initially developed in high-income countries, a central challenge is therefore to determine its value and appropriateness for South Africa and other low-income countries. Given that violence in urban areas has complex causes, and that this complexity increases with a decrease in income (Mohan, 1996), this framework cannot simply be transposed onto the South African context. The public health framework essentially argues that the principles that are utilized with communicable and non-communicable diseases can also be applied with regards to the control and prevention of violence (Butchart, 1996). These principles are most commonly articulated through the four steps of public health, including problem definition, risk factor identification, developing and testing interventions, and evaluating their effectiveness in order to diffuse and replicate practices. However, the medical origin of this model has resulted in a strong reliance on a quantitative disease framework that attempts to define public health problems (such as violence) epidemiologically and to identify determinants, risks and triggers temporally (Haddon & Baker, 1981). This approach does not easily allow for an overt ideological, political and social analysis of violence and its consequent prevention (e.g., the distinction between intentional and unintentional violence does not adequately account for many micro- and macro-level processes that contribute to climates of violence). Furthermore, it has traditionally functioned as a deficit model that tends to underplay the importance of community resilience. Whilst local communities are certainly targeted within this framework, the improvement in the overall health status of entire populations is emphasized. Also, public health practitioners have historically preferred passive rather than active interventions which reduce the focus on bottom-up community participation in favor of a top-down policy formulation (Butchart & Kruger, 2001; Stevens, Wyngaard & van Niekerk, 2001).

A community development approach on the other hand, attempts to harness organic knowledges, resources, skills, resiliences and assets in the process of re-empowering 'disempowered' communities. Despite the internal diversity of perspectives (see, for example, the work of Seedat, Duncan & Lazarus, 2001), it is a framework that relies on collective needs assessments, participatory research processes and action-oriented interventions that encourage community mobilization, self-reliance and capacitation. It is premised upon a democratic philosophy that values equal partnerships forged between practitioners and community members. It is much more locally focused and tends to favor bottom-up processes that involve action towards social change in historically fragmented and disadvantaged contexts. This is an essential component for developing grassroots forms of transformation in societies in transition from structural oppression to democracy. This framework aims to critically assess communities' overall psychosocial status and to promote conscious and informed social action to improve this status (Scedat, Duncan & Lazarus, 2001).

Despite the apparent differences between these approaches, a distillation and fusion of their central elements is certainly possible to produce a comprehensive violence prevention matrix for research and intervention in disempowered, under-resourced communities. This integration requires the act of becoming reflexive about methodologies and the conceptualization of health and social issues. One of the most powerful conduits to achieve this is to critically consider the assumptions underpinning the construction of interventions.

Western understandings of health and social issues, such as those within the traditional public health model, have historically been imposed on people from different contexts.[2]

If practitioners were to be unreflective about imposing this methodology, community knowledges and macro-political realities would be elided. On the other hand, it is naive to assert that interventions can be implemented without imposing externally derived theoretical, epistemological, ontological, and methodological assumptions on the local context. Such an approach would invalidate and minimize practitioners' valuable contributions to interventions by ignoring the rich possibilities of dialectical interactions with communities. The challenge remains to construct interventions that permit the emergence and validation of organic community knowledges, whilst not devaluing the knowledges brought to bear on communities by practitioners. This task involves a process of the co-construction and negotiation of research and intervention strategies (Jahoda, 1995; Kim & Berry, 1993; Swartz, 1998).

One of the ways in which the limitations of utilizing the public health approach to violence prevention in the South African context can be offset, is through infusing this approach with a community development perspective. The four basic steps of the public health approach are sufficiently broad to accommodate for social scientific processes that involve data collection, analysis, theory-testing and the generation of new knowledges (Bhana & Kanjee, 2001). In essence, this implies that the public health principles of problem definition, risk factor identification, developing and testing interventions, and evaluating their effectiveness in order to diffuse practices that may be implemented in a more widespread and replicable manner, may also be applied to social scientific processes of research and interventions. Community development approaches as action-oriented forms of participatory social scientific inquiry, involve an emphasis on community constructions of violence, as well as mobilizing participation in research and interventions. The fusion of the public health and community development approaches is therefore advantageous for several reasons. Firstly, it maximizes potential knowledge resources for the purposes of good practice research and service delivery methodologies. Despite the epistemological, ontological and methodological slant of the public health model, in its adapted form, it represents a matrix for violence prevention research and interventions that allows for the conscious incorporation of alternative epistemologies, ontologies and methodologies. Secondly, it facilitates sectoral, intersectoral and interdisciplinary coalition-building by bringing together a range of stakeholders that are imperative to addressing the complexities of violence as a social phenomenon (Butchart & Emmett, 2000). At the same time, it accommodates for the specialized expertise that each discipline or sectoral component has to offer in understanding and preventing violence. Thirdly, it promotes the value of more participatory, illuminative and qualitative approaches, as well as traditional public health research and intervention methods. The latter includes epidemiology, ongoing surveillance of violence patterns, risk factor analyses, educative interventions, environmental modifications, engineering strategies, enforcement, and ongoing monitoring and evaluation of the efficacy and impact of these interventions. This degree of plurality enhances the overall methodological rigor of initiatives and facilitates evidence-led interventions that may be thoroughly evaluated and refined accordingly (Bhana & Kanjee, 2001).

At a theoretical level, contextual social analyses complement more technical analyses of specific antecedents and consequences of violence. Violence can therefore be addressed at a macro-level as well as at the levels of individuals, families and communities. This permits the possibility of moving beyond the restrictive definitions of violence that are situation and event specific (Haddon & Baker, 1981), to include political and ideological components that help to contextualize this phenomenon (Bulhan, 1985). Finally, this framework values bottom-up and top-down approaches equally. In so doing, formal and indigenous knowledges are both given voice, with passive and active interventions aimed at structural change being encouraged (Stevens et al., 2001). However, despite this potential interdisciplinarity, theoretical diversity and methodological pluralism, such an adapted matrix cannot be implemented successfully without conscious community participation, empowerment, capacitation and mobilization.

EVALUATING THE CAPACITY OF THE MATRIX IN THE CONTEXT OF A NEIGHBORHOOD-BASED VIOLENCE PREVENTION INITIATIVE

The following section represents a specific example of the pilot application of the above-outlined approach to violence prevention within a community and aims to stimulate critical thought about prevention in communities. The initiative involved a multi-focused community intervention that entailed primary, secondary and tertiary prevention initiatives implemented at multiple sites. By simultaneously targeting violence at different levels, a more comprehensive community impact was anticipated.

The initiative was piloted in a low-income community 20 kilometers south-west of the metropolis of Johannesburg. Historically, this community was established in the 1960s as part of the apartheid government's policy of separate development, through the forced removals of people with the implementation of the Group Areas Act of 1950.[3] Whilst the contemporary community composition is not homogenous, most inhabitants could be described as working class or unemployed.

The inequalities of the apartheid system of governance remain reflected within the community's poor infrastructural and economic development, seen in the high unemployment levels, poor physical environments, limited communication and transport infrastructures, housing shortages, inadequate educational and recreational facilities, and related social problems such as alcoholism, gangsterism, racism and domestic violence.

Step One of the Adapted Matrix

Several years of consistent violence prevention work yielded a range of experientially based understandings of the most significant challenges being faced by this community. Qualitative as well as quantitative and epidemiological studies conducted with targeted sectors of the population confirmed that violence was a significant obstacle to community development. In addition, a review of the available national and provincial statistical data on violence highlighted the magnitude of this phenomenon as a contributor to death and disability, and served as useful contextual information within which to locate the local data. Initial community responses to feedback were mixed, with some viewing the findings as legitimate and others reflecting a degree of trepidation. This was particularly so, given that prior to 1994 many disadvantaged communities attempted to define themselves in terms of their assets, rather than their deficits.

It also indicated that more comprehensive data on the challenges facing the community needed to be collected in an inclusive and participatory manner. Data collection and coalition-building became a programmatic priority during this period.

After consulting with local government authorities, service deliverers and key knowledge brokers in the community, household surveys of several representative neighborhoods were conducted. Community volunteers were trained, capacitated and integrally involved in the data collection (both quantitative and qualitative). In addition, school-going youth were also targeted as a significant cohort from which to access information. A collaborative qualitative study was undertaken in schools and comprised transect walks with learners and educators to indicate areas of danger and safety on school premises, focus group discussions with learners and educators, and finally, a youth risk behavior survey. Selected learners validated the data and provided feedback to their respective schools. This constituted sufficient baseline data that brought with it the necessary community participation and legitimacy. Contributions from several disciplines were used in the data collection and problem definition phase to provide expertise on methodologies, accessing strategies, community mapping, coalition building, etc. These included psychology, anthropology, sociology, epidemiology, bio-statistics, social policy and public health.

Step Two of the Adapted Matrix

While descriptive qualitative and quantitative data was critical to defining the nature, magnitude and extent of the challenges to community development, more analytical processes were required to determine causal relationships, risk factors, proximal and distal triggers and resilience factors. This phase allowed for even greater methodological and theoretical diversity to be brought to bear on the initial understandings of the challenges facing the community. For example, qualitative techniques (such as focus groups, interviews and thematic analyses) were utilized to determine the meanings youth associated with sexual violence. In addition, statistical analyses were conducted to determine the risks and resiliences associated with sexual coercion. At a community level, risks for childhood injuries were also assessed. Furthermore, the extent to which participation, training and capacitation among community volunteers improved knowledge retention on safety, attitudinal change, behavioral change, and overall resiliency in the face of exposure to community violence and structural risk factors was assessed. Finally, attempts to disaggregate data on homicide for this community to determine the macro-, meso- and micro-level determinants of this form of violence were initiated. Complementing this, participatory action research was undertaken to help understand the social constructions associated with homicide. Here again, this phase included inputs from a variety of disciplines in the social and health sciences and key community stakeholders and role-players. Feedback was provided to community members, policy-makers, local authorities and service deliverers in this community. This phase strengthened interdisciplinarity within the intervention, consolidated community participation and 'buy-in,' and allowed for a more focused development of intervention strategies aimed at addressing risks and harnessing resiliences.

Step Three of the Adapted Matrix

The primary objectives of this phase were to focus on high-risk environments, groups and behaviors and to structure primary, secondary and tertiary prevention initiatives. By introducing this type of multiple intervention strategy within a community, there existed a greater potential to generate capacity beyond individual 'human capital' to promoting the development of 'social capital.' After reviewing the extant national and international literature on good practices for violence prevention, interventions were adapted to accommodate local knowledges and the uniqueness of the South African context. The interventions initiated were based on identified community needs (step one) and risks (step two). These included (1) a primary prevention schools-based intervention directed towards learners and educators to improve overall safety, (2) a primary prevention home-visitation program to enhance household safety and to facilitate violence prevention within homes, (3) a primary prevention social support intervention aimed at reducing structural risk-factors for violence, such as unemployment and poverty, (4) a secondary preventative intervention involving the provision of psychosocial after-care for victims of violence, and (5) a tertiary preventative intervention aimed at promoting home-based after-care and rehabilitation for victims of violence.

Each of these interventions involved partnerships with relevant sectors of the community and differing levels of direct service delivery. In some instances, direct service delivery was central, whilst in others, networks and collaborations were favored. Integral to all of these interventions was the ongoing development, refinement and evaluation of participatory methodologies for the purposes of diffusion and replication.

The *Schools-Based Intervention* aimed to promote a culture of learning through the prevention and reduction of violence, and the promotion of safe and healthy behavioral repertoires among school-going youth. Schools-based interventions have been successfully implemented in a range of national and international contexts, and are particularly valuable insofar as they provide a captive audience of youth within a relatively structured and resourced environment (Morojele, Knott, Myburg & Finkelstein, 1998; Stephens, 1998). Whilst it included aspects of secondary prevention, it was predominantly a primary prevention initiative. It included monitoring violence at schools through ongoing surveillance and behavioral surveys (to complement the activities of step one), leadership training for youth, psycho-educational programs to address violence, and overall safety planning and management. The intervention involved learners, educators, parents and other community role-players to varying degrees. Whilst this intervention included direct service delivery, networks with other service deliverers better suited to directing specific aspects of the intervention were facilitated. Importantly, the central aspects of this intervention were also reflexively evaluated at a process and design level, and modified accordingly.

The *Home-Visitation Program* also had several primary and secondary prevention objectives that included assessing and monitoring levels of violence within homes, providing physically present home visitors who forged relationships with community members, and served an educative and information dissemination role (around safety, health and welfare). Finally, the repeated contacts with community members in their households acted as a deterrent for spousal and/or child abuse and neglect.[4] Unemployed community volunteers who had been extensively trained in safety promotion, formed the backbone of this intervention. Given the potentially important contribution that community-based volunteers can make in low-income, under-resourced communities, seeking formal recognition for these community-based service deliverers was an active component of the intervention. In this regard, linkages between volunteers and local government were facilitated and nurtured in an attempt to incentivize the volunteer work by obtaining local government subsidization (e.g., reduction in taxes, school fees, etc.). Here again, this intervention allowed for the interface between the community, trained volunteers, service deliverers and elements from several disciplines. In addition, evaluation was central to this intervention and preliminary qualitative information indicated that the volunteers were more resilient in the face of exposure to violence and were being identified as resources by the community.

The *Social Support Intervention* was a primary prevention initiative that attempted to offset the structural risk factors of unemployment and poverty within this historically 'racialised' and disadvantaged community. It ultimately promoted partnerships between community members who were interested in small business development and entrepreneurship as a means of self-employment, and organizations specifically focused on this (see strategies of the Department of Trade and Industry, 1995). After facilitating these partnerships, the evaluation strategy involved the documentation of the social histories of members and their progression through the intervention, and whether participation decreased the likelihood of exposure to violence. Here again, coalition-building with community members, external agencies and other disciplines (e.g., economics) illustrated potentially creative ways of marshalling resources from diverse sectors for violence prevention within communities.

The *Psychosocial After-Care* intervention focused on the provision of appropriate secondary prevention services for victims of violence in an attempt to reduce its impact (WHO, 2001). This intervention was driven by health workers who contributed their expertise and time at several sites and helped to foster positive institutional relationships within the service delivery sector of the community. It also highlighted the need for the development of appropriate short-term modalities to address the psychosocial aftermath of violence. In addition to trauma counseling, it involved the training of community counselors and evaluations of psychosocial service delivery within this area, to improve overall service delivery for victims of violence (e.g., medico-legal services dealing with rape survivors). As with the previous initiatives, this intervention also drew together community members, service deliverers (e.g., the police and health workers) as well as researcher-practitioners in the health and social sciences.

The *Home-Based After-Care* for victims of violence initiative was a tertiary prevention strategy aimed at the control of the impact of violence through the provision of home-based after-care. This was particularly critical in instances where health and rehabilitation services were inaccessible to members of communities because of physical distance, lack of financial resources or health care resources. This initiative was also driven by community volunteers and though in its formative stages, built on their existing knowledge of safety, violence prevention and health promotion, so that they could deliver services to community members. Secondary and tertiary prevention initiatives play an important role in reducing the potential mortality and morbidity of violence and therefore, represent crucial complementary strategies to primary prevention initiatives (Werner & Sanders, 1997; WHO, 2001). Once again, community volunteers participated in training offered by health workers to ensure that quality indicators of care were met. The central evaluation strategy of this intervention was to assess the effectiveness of volunteers in this capacity, but also to cost this initiative, so as to lobby for resources to be allocated to volunteers who fulfill crucial health care functions.

Step Four of the Adapted Matrix

The final phase of this adapted approach encompassed evaluation and diffusion of good practice information pertaining to research and service delivery. Given that this was a pilot program, impact assessment would have been premature, but preliminary process and design evaluations appeared promising. However, what remained critical was to determine the degree to which these interventions had holistically contributed to the prevention, reduction and control of violence and its sequelae, and the degree to which they had contributed to fostering the development of community skills, empowerment, cohesion, trust, etc. (i.e., 'social capital'). At other levels, the objectives of this phase were met through the implementation of advocacy campaigns, predominantly by community members and through community mobilization. Lobbying was integral to the volunteer-driven interventions, and proved successful enough to generate financial sustainability and minimize group attrition. In addition, policy briefs were formulated to recommend changes to current medico-legal facilities. Based on the school interventions, advocacy documents highlighting the challenges facing youth and educators as well as emergent schools-based good practices in violence prevention in South Africa were produced. This also formed part of an ongoing lobbying process to provincial government to infuse safety promotion and violence prevention further into school activities. Finally, research results and initial program evaluation outcomes were diffused through seminars, popular media, academic publications, formal and informal courses, policy briefs, and stakeholder meetings.

CONCLUSION

Emerging from the above, it is apparent that the fusion of public health and community development principles is not only possible, but is also desirable in the prevention of violence within communities. This adapted framework represents a matrix through which to consciously engage in community prevention work on a number of specific psychosocial and health-related challenges, and simultaneously accommodates for theoretical diversity, methodological pluralism, interdisciplinarity and the philosophy and principles of community development. It also allows for evidence-led interventions to be structured across micro-, meso- and macro-levels; with universal, targeted and specified populations and environments; and at primary, secondary and tertiary levels.

However, it is important to note that this adapted matrix is not underpinned by a generic scientific neutrality that automatically accommodates for diverse philosophical foundations of science, but rather, that it allows for the conscious co-existence of varying ontologies, epistemologies and methodologies in the prevention of violence. The key element in this process is therefore the *conscious* introduction of alternative and complimentary perspectives of science and their application to the resolution of obstacles to health and psychosocial well-being within communities. This is particularly important to emphasize, given the erroneous belief that the public health model is in and of itself an all-encompassing and scientifically neutral framework able to accommodate for a range of diverse perspectives.

In addition, this adapted matrix does not circumvent many of the inherent tensions, contradictions and challenges facing those involved in preventative work within low-income, under-resourced communities. Continuous processes of negotiation between formal academic knowledges and organic indigenous knowledges are imperative; managing leadership tensions and vested interests within ever-changing communities is crucial to ensuring organizational integrity and legitimacy; perceptively responding to perceived levels of capacitation or incapacitation amongst community members is critical to intervention success; and nurturing partnerships and collaborations between a wider range of stakeholders and role-players becomes even more central to successful implementation and sustainability. Furthermore, complex, ecologically-based interventions such as the one reflected upon in this article raise their own challenges with regard to evaluation, cost-effectiveness and sustainability. Here, the importance of highly specific and focused project conceptualization for each element of the intervention, mixed evaluation methods (such as empowerment evaluations and randomized control trials), and critical costing methodologies that balance community needs and financial constraints become imperative challenges to address and integrate into programs. Finally, organizational roles and histories should not be underestimated as factors that determine the success or failure of interventions. Questions relating to the importance of a vision-keeper organization within this process, as well as the long-term commitment of organizations and funders to communities are critical to interrogate as potential factors that enhance sustainability through long-term coalition and relationship-building, as they may ultimately contribute to the flourishing of initiatives such as these.

Nevertheless, this matrix provides a starting point that may enable preventionists to marshal a wide range of resources within an overarching framework that is flexible, yet structured and focused enough to facilitate comprehensive and holistic prevention work within communities. The framework ultimately aims to accommodate for interdisciplinarity, methodological pluralism and theoretical diversity as we attempt to build coalitions within a philosophy of community empowerment.

NOTES

1. Human capital and social capital are development concepts that refer to the degree of existing individual or community resources within contexts of poverty and minimal resources (see for example, Emmett, 2000; Moser, 1997). They are seemingly asset-based notions of development, but are derived from neo-liberal ideologies and discourses that place the emphasis on individuals and communities in addressing economic underdevelopment and are therefore placed in inverted commas to highlight this problematic.

2. This tendency has been criticized by writers in the fields of cultural and cross-cultural psychology, drawing on what is known as the etic-emic distinction. The term etic is used to describe a universalistic approach, which imposes a particular worldview, and emphasizes what is presumed to be typical of all people across contexts. The term emic, by contrast, emphasizes the importance of indigenous, local knowledges, and the uniqueness of human experience framed by cultural and contex-

tual influences. Theoretical assumptions underpinning research and interventions are often presumed to be etic without question, instead of being acknowledged as Euro-American emics, pseudo-etics, or what has also been referred to as imposed etics (Jahoda, 1995; Kim & Berry, 1993; Swartz, 1998).

3. This Act allowed for the legal residential segregation of the population according to the 'racially' defined label assigned to them by the apartheid regime. Miscegenation was therefore totally prohibited, especially at a residential level.

4. This is a known outcome of Home-Visitation Programs and has been shown to reduce the incidence of child abuse and neglect, which is in itself a risk factor for anti-social behaviour among adolescents (Mohamed, 2001).

REFERENCES

Ahmed, A. & Pretorius-Heuchert, J.W. (2001). Notions of social change in community psychology: Issues and challenges. In M. Seedat, N. Duncan & S. Lazarus (Eds.), *Theory, method and practice in community psychology: South African and other perspectives* (pp. 67-85). Cape Town: Oxford University Press.

Bhana, A. & Kanjee, A. (2001). Epistemological and methodological issues in community psychology. In M. Seedat, N. Duncan & S. Lazarus (Eds.), *Theory, method and practice in community psychology: South African and other perspectives* (pp. 135-158). Cape Town: Oxford University Press.

Bond, P. (1994). RDP versus World Bank. *International Viewpoint*, No. 257, 16-17.

Bond, P. (2000). *Elite transition*. London: Pluto Press.

Bulhan, H.A. (1985). *Frantz Fanon and the psychology of oppression*. New York: Plenum Press.

Burrows, S. (2000). Understanding suicide in South Africa. *ISHS Monograph Series*, 2(3), (pp. 37-52).

Burrows, S., Bowman, B., Matzopoulos, R. & van Niekerk, A. (2001). *A profile of fatal injuries in South Africa 2000*. Tygerberg: Medical Research Council.

Butchart, A. (1996). Violence prevention in Gauteng: The public health approach. *Acta Criminologica*, 9(2), 5-15.

Butchart, A. & Emmett, T. (2000). Crime, violence and public health. In T. Emmet & A. Butchart (Eds.), *Behind the mask* (pp. 3-28). Pretoria: HSRC.

Butchart, A., Nell, V. & Seedat, M. (1996). Violence in South Africa: Its definition and prevention as a public health problem. In J. Seager and C. Parry (Eds.), *Urbanization and health in South Africa* (pp. 1-41). Tygerberg: Medical Research Council.

Butchart, A. & Kruger, J. (2001). Public health and community psychology: A case study in community-based injury prevention. In M. Seedat, N. Duncan & S. Lazarus (Eds.), *Theory, method and practice in community psychology: South African and other perspectives* (pp. 215-241). Cape Town: Oxford University Press.

Dawes, A. (1990). The effects of political violence on children: A consideration of South African and related studies. *International Journal of Psychology*, 25, 13-31.

Department of Trade and Industry (1995). *National strategy for the development and promotion of small business in South Africa: White paper of the Department of Trade and Industry*. Pretoria: Government Printer.

Duncan, N. & Rock, B. (1994). *Inquiry into the effects of public violence on children: Preliminary report.* Sandton: Goldstone Commission.

Emmett, T. (2000). Addressing the underlying causes of crime and violence in South Africa. In T. Emmet & A. Butchart (Eds.), *Behind the mask* (pp. 273-332). Pretoria: HSRC.

Emmett, T. & Butchart, A. (2000). (Eds.). *Behind the mask.* Pretoria: HSRC.

Fitzgerald, P. (1995). (Ed.). *Managing sustainable development in South Africa.* Cape Town: Oxford University Press.

Haddon, W. & Baker, S. (1981). Injury control. In D. Clark & C. MacMahon (Eds.), *Preventive and community medicine* (pp. 109-140). Boston: Little Brown and Company.

Jahoda, G. (1995). In pursuit of the emic-etic distinction: Can we ever capture it? In N.R. Goldberger & J.B. Veroff (Eds.), *The culture and psychology reader* (pp. 128-138). New York: New York University Press.

Kim, U. & Berry, J.W. (1993). Introduction. In U. Kim & J.W. Berry (Eds.), *Indigenous psychologies: Research experience in cultural context* (pp. 1-29). Newbury Park: Sage.

Mohamed, F. (2001). Considerations in designing a volunteer home-visitation program in low-income, at-risk communities: A review of the literature. *ISHS Monograph Series, 2*(4), 64-81.

Mohan, D. (1996). Control of injuries in large cities: Dealing with plurality and complexity. *Karolinska Institutet summary of international congress, Safe Communities: The Application to Large Urban Environments,* November 14-16. Dallas, Texas, USA.

Morojele, N., Knott, R., Myburg, H. & Finkelstein, N. (1998). Audit of school-based prevention programs in the Western Cape. *Urban Health and Development Bulletin.*

Moser, C. (1997). *Poverty reduction in South Africa. The importance of household relations and social capital as assets of the poor.* Unpublished report, The World Bank, Washington DC.

Pretorius-Heuchert, J.W. & Ahmed, A. (2001). Community psychology: Past, present and future. In M. Seedat, N. Duncan & S. Lazarus (Eds.), *Theory, method and practice in community psychology: South African and other perspectives* (pp. 17-36). Cape Town: Oxford University Press.

Schonteich, M. (1999). *Assessing the crime fighters: The ability of the criminal justice system to solve and prosecute crime.* Pretoria: Institute for Security Studies.

Seedat, M. (1995). Creating safe communities in the context of reconstruction and development: The Center for Peace Action. *Psychosocial Research and Practice, 2,* 27-32.

Seedat, M., Duncan, N. & Lazarus, S. (Eds.) (2001). *Community psychology. Theory, method and practice.* Cape Town: Oxford University Press.

Stephens, R.D. (1998). Safe schools planning. In D.S. Elliot, B.A. Hamburg and K.R. Williams (Eds.), *Violence in American schools* (pp. 253-292). New York: Cambridge University Press.

Stevens, G. (2000). Marginalised youth in South Africa: Crisis or conversion? *ISHS Monograph Series, 1*(4), 4-53.

Stevens, G., Wyngaard, G. & van Niekerk, A. (2001). The safe schools model: An antidote to school violence? *Perspectives in Education, 19*(2), 145-158.

Straker, G. (1992). *Faces in the revolution.* Cape Town: David Phillip.

Swartz, L. (1998). *Culture and mental health: A Southern African view.* Cape Town: Oxford University Press.

Werner, D. & Sanders, D. (1997). *Questioning the solution.* Palo Alto: HealthWrights.

WHO (2001). *Proceedings of WHO meeting to develop a 5-year strategy. Unpublished document WHO/NMH/VIP/01.04.* Geneva: Department of Injuries and Violence Prevention, World Health Organization.

The Use of Public Health Research in Stimulating Violence and Injury Prevention Practices and Policies: Reflections from South Africa

Mohamed Seedat
Anabela Nascimento

University of South Africa

SUMMARY. There is a paucity of academic work examining the applicability and utility of epidemiological data in efforts to inform injury prevention policy and practice. Drawing on experiences from two South

Mohamed Seedat (D. Phil.) is a clinical psychologist and is professor and director of the Institute for Social and Health Sciences. He is the editor of *Community Psychology. Theory, Method and Practice.* Cape Town: Oxford University Press.

Anabela Nascimento (D. Phil.) is a counseling psychologist.

Address correspondence to: Mohamed Seedat, Institute for Social and Health Sciences & Crime, Violence and Injury Lead Program (MRC-UNISA), University of South Africa, P.O. Box 1087, Lenasia 1820, South Africa (E-mail address: SEEDAMA@unisa.ac.za) (M.A. Seedat).

An earlier version of this paper was presented at Forum 5. The 10/90 Gap in Health Research: Assessing the Progress. Geneva (11-12 October, 2001).

The authors thank all those who participated in the individual and focus group discussions. A special thanks to Adele Kirsten, Claire Taylor, Melvyn Freeman, Natalie Mayet, Prema Naidoo, Shan Bolton, and Dr. Shan Naidoo for their incisive contributions.

[Haworth co-indexing entry note]: "The Use of Public Health Research in Stimulating Violence and Injury Prevention Practices and Policies: Reflections from South Africa." Seedat, Mohamed, and Anabela Nascimento. Co-published simultaneously in *Journal of Prevention & Intervention in the Community* (The Haworth Press, Inc.) Vol. 25. No. 1, 2003, pp. 31-47; and: *Prevention and Intervention Practice in Post-Apartheid South Africa* (ed: Vijé Franchi; cons. ed: Norman Duncan) The Haworth Press. Inc., 2003, pp. 31-47.

African case examples we explore the utility of injury surveillance and epidemiological data, and review the contextual, content, process and social actor related factors that influence prevention policy reform and practices. In addition to a responsive socio-political environment, personal relationships, researcher credibility, institutional capacity, careful data packaging, ongoing dissemination, pressure from civil society, and the formation of alliances are among the many significant factors influencing the uptake of injury data and associated prevention policy and practice initiatives. By way of conclusion, we raise the importance of developing strategies to minimize the misuse of empirically generated data. *[Article copies available for a fee from The Haworth Document Delivery Service: 1-800-HAWORTH. E-mail address: <docdelivery@haworthpress.com> Website: <http://www.HaworthPress.com> © 2003 by The Haworth Press, Inc. All rights reserved.]*

KEYWORDS. Injury data, policy implications, utility, uptake

INTRODUCTION

Most public health researchers who produce injury epidemiological and surveillance data do so for the purposes of informing injury prevention and containment policies and practices (Butchart, 1999; Laflamme, Eilert-Petersen, & Schelp, 1999). However, the assumption that quality injury data may be translated coherently and dynamically into empirical platforms for the facilitation of significant injury prevention practices and policies remains untested. There is a paucity of studies elucidating the processes and challenges involved in attempts to encourage injury data uptake within the prevention sector.

Disciplines such as community psychology have recognized the strategic importance of engaging in policy-related work (Lazarus, 2001). Several writers therefore suggest that research may be used to inform and influence agenda formulation, policy discussions, the associated policy formulation and implementation processes, and evaluate the impact of new or existing legislation and related policies (Jason, 1991; Lazarus, 2001; Solarz, 1995).

In tracing the initial application of the South African National Injury Mortality Surveillance System (NIMSS) data, Burrows (2001) established that the use of the data varied according to the focus and needs of user-groups, including non-governmental organizations (NGOs) and government departments. Even though at least 50 well-placed end-user groups in the injury prevention sector are on record as having utilized the data for purposes of public awareness, education, prevention and policy advocacy, in the main the data remains under-utilized.

In a study of health care financing reforms in South Africa and Zambia, Gilson, Doherty, Mcintyre et al. (1999), drawing on the policy analysis literature, suggest that the reform policy process is influenced by factors concerning context, content, process and social actors. *Contextual* factors may include socio-economic structures, the socio-cultural values and commitments of society, and the objective conditions at a specific moment in the society's history. *Content* issues may relate to the nature, structure and design of suggested reforms, and the relationship with other parallel institutional developments. *Process* elements focus on the manner in which reforms are identified, defined and implemented, and include matters of consultation, timing, and phasing. Social *actor* factors refer to beliefs and vested interests that operate to shape and influence policy reform work.

Ultimately, policy-making and implementation is a complex socio-political and institutionalized act for which decision-makers may utilize single or multiple sources of information (Lazarus, 2001). The various sources are summarized in Figure 1, extracted from the Gilson et al. study (1999). Within such an information matrix, independent routine epidemiological and surveillance data may be critical for informing, monitoring and evaluating the development, implementation and adaptation of public health policies and associated practices.

FIGURE 1. Sources of Information for Governmental Decision-Making Adapted from the Gilson et al. Study (1999)

Formal Sources	
(1) • Departmental research/inquiry • Internal think-tank report • Reports from internal experts	(2) • Commissions • Committees of inquiry • Judicial review • Reports from the legislature • Commissioned research • Formal consultation
Sources internal to	*Sources external to*
the Government	*the Government*
• Informal discussions between decision-makers • Gossip/rumour • Informal use of advisers	• Discussions • Consultation • Reports • Informal information/advice
(4)	(3)
Informal Sources	

Public policy reform and development is a political process often characterized by contest and conflict. Bowe and Ball (1992, cited in Lazarus, 2001) refer to three important sources of influence on policy development, namely (1) the context of influence, (2) the context of policy production, and (3) the context of practice. Whereas the context of influence refers to the milieu within which social policy may be initiated, the context of policy production refers to the production of materials of relevance to the policy. These materials could include policy documents, media reports, speeches by significant social actors and official legal documents. The context of practice deals with the interpretation of policy documents and the translation of such interpretation into practice. The dynamics of policy formulation and development require careful consideration. Space constraints do not permit a detailed review of such dynamics here. Suffice it to indicate that it is vital for researchers operating in the social policy arena to link to the justice arena so as to understand the legislative process. The American Psychological Association, for instance, provides good guidelines to assist researchers to engage the legislative process in the United States (Lazarus, 2001; Rickel, 1993). In South Africa initial ideas and proposals are usually presented to the public in the form of white papers, which are followed by public hearings and written submissions, which in turn inform the development of laws. Following the establishment of a legal framework, specific rules and regulations are developed to guide the promulgation of the laws (Lazarus, 2001).

PURPOSE AND AIMS

Following these aforementioned considerations, our purpose is to examine how and under what circumstances surveillance and epidemiology data are used to inform injury prevention policy and practice in South Africa. More specifically, by way of two detailed case reviews we aim to chart the factors related to context, content, process and social actors that serve to influence and maximize the utility of such data. Below we proceed with a brief overview of the South African health policy context and a description of the NIMSS initiative and the three neighborhood safety promotion study.

THE SOUTH AFRICAN HEALTH POLICY CONTEXT

Following the formal dismantling of political apartheid and the first democratic elections in 1994, health policy has undergone significant reorientation, intended to facilitate the development of a comprehensive integrated national health system that can provide accessible health services to all South Africans. Consistent with World Health Organization (WHO) recommendations, health policy has shifted towards developing and strengthening preventive primary health care. De-emphasizing curative tertiary medicine, the focus in primary care is on the prevention of illness and injury through immunization, education, and safe hygienic, dietary and behavioral practices (Stack & Ndletyana, 2001). Even though injury and violence prevention do not feature within this priority listing the South African government is party to the 1996 forty-ninth World Health Assembly resolution (WHA 94.25), which declared violence to be a major public health problem (WHA, 1996). Debates and shifts in health policy are likely to be influenced substantially by the government's present macro-economic policies, the associated move away from the Reconstruction and Development Program (RDP), and the encroaching debilitating and facilitative influences of current-day globalization. The RDP, in which the state was defined as the coordinator of development, represented an intention to redress apartheid-generated economic and social inequalities through re-distribution, a people-centered development process, and a range of high-profile Presidential Lead Projects, a few of which were situated within the Department of Health (Gilson, Doherty, Mcintyre et al., 1999; Innes, 1997). In contrast to the national priorities and demands placed on the post-apartheid state, globalization tends to de-emphasize the role of the nation-state in social development, and uphold the virtues of economic liberation and privatization, and so encourages cuts in social spending. The proliferating influence of the World Bank's policies, which stress the "privatization and marketization of health services" (Larkin, 1998, p. 104), cost-effective programming and a diminished role for the state, are therefore likely to impact on the South African equity-oriented health policy frameworks (Larkin, 1998; Nabudere, 2000).

INJURY DATA INITIATIVES AND METHODOLOGY

The South African National Violence and Injury Surveillance System

In 1998 the South African Department of Arts, Culture, Science and Technology (DACST), through a R2.5 million grant enabled the establishment of a national violence and injury surveillance system. The aims of the surveillance system are to: (1) produce reliable descriptive epidemiological data for the estimated 65,000 non-natural deaths that occur annually; (2) produce representative descriptive epidemiological data for the estimated three million non-fatal injury cases registered annually, using a method of sentinel sampling; and (3) trace patterns of alcohol and drug use among newly injured victims through regular cross-sectoral surveys (Burrows, 2001; Butchart, 1999).

Underlying these broad aims, the surveillance initiative is intended to inform the design, implementation, monitoring, evaluation and financing of injury prevention and control programs (Laflamme, Eilert-Petersen & Schelp, 1999; Mercy, Ikeda & Powell, 1998; WHO, 1999).

One part of the injury surveillance system, the National Injury Mortality Surveillance System (NIMSS), was piloted in 1998 and formalized in 1999. As of April 2002, coverage was estimated to be at 34 percent of all non-natural deaths occurring in South Africa. During the 2000 to 2001 period, lead researchers on the project invested a fair amount of resources to produce and circulate quarterly, annual and customized reports to various end-users (Buehler, 1998; Burrows, 2001; Declich & Carter, 1994).

Methodology

A review of the NIMSS records in August 2001 indicated that at least fifty (50) end-users, including public health administrators, researchers, advocacy and lobbyist groups, forensic pathologists, media and service providers were recipients of the 1999 annual mortality surveillance report. A multi data collection method was utilized to solicit information from these recipients who represented a convenience sample. The data collection methods included telephonic and face-to-face interviews, focus group discussions and a review of documents. We also conducted an extensive case review with Gun-Free South Africa (GFSA), an NGO working to promote gun free zones and stricter gun-control laws in South Africa. We conducted the case review to examine the specific organizational and socio-political factors that encouraged linkages between research, policy and practice. Gun-Free South Africa utilized the 1999 annual mortality surveillance report during significant phases of its gun-control campaign and in submissions to parliamentary hearings.

The Three Neighborhood Safety Promotion Study

Following the logic of "local data for local action," the Three Neighborhood Safety Promotion Study was initiated in 1994 (Butchart &

Kruger, 2001). The study delineated the intervention population as all residents within the geographical boundaries of Eldorado Park, a township south-west of Johannesburg, historically reserved for those classified as "coloured" in the apartheid nomenclature, and which includes several informal settlements where the residents are mainly black-African.

Aside from profiling the demographic and environmental characteristics of the area, the study succeeded in producing information on the injury incidence rate per 100,000 population, and the injury mortality rate for the sample. Researchers on the study also produced data on the distribution of injury causes by age and gender, and identified alcohol, over-crowding, proximity to busy highways, and poor overall environmental conditions as significant risk factors for injury. The overall findings were subsequently used to suggest specific injury prevention activities in a submission to the Johannesburg Southern Metropolitan Council, which was the local municipal authority responsible for health and safety promotion within and around the catchment area of Eldorado Park.

Methodology

In order to establish the utility of the report we conducted individual in-depth face-to-face interviews with three political figures and two public health administrators who were attached to the former Southern Metropolitan Local Council (SMLC) at the time that the injury report was presented.

FINDINGS

In this section we organize the findings to answer three key questions: (1) How and why were the injury epidemiology and surveillance data utilized? (2) Which specific context, content, process and actor factors encouraged GFSA and the SMLC to use the data? and (3) What are the emerging lessons for injury epidemiologists seeking to maximize the utility of their data in contexts where science is often regarded with skepticism?

Why and By Whom Was NIMSS Data Utilized?

Our results echo the findings of the Burrows (2001) unpublished study. The NIMSS data were used for: (1) education and public debate; (2) policy advocacy and reform; (3) management decisions; (4) research, teaching and training; (5) strengthening commitments to implement legislation; (6) building alliances; (7) justifying and lobbying for new projects; (8) academic and media presentations; and (9) initiating and funding projects (see Table 1).

As a management tool, forensic pathologists, for instance, used NIMSS reports to ascertain caseloads, refine recording procedures and justify budget requests. Groups such as the Council for Scientific and Industrial Research (CSIR) and Emergency Services also used NIMSS data to modify or extend their programmatic orientation to include prevention activities. As an educational tool data were used to draw public attention to the patterns and distribution of injuries and GFSA, for example, encouraged fellow agencies to use the data for programmatic design and strategic planning. As part of the public educational campaign, the NIMSS data sometimes served to generate debate around gun control. The National Directorate for Mental Health and Substance Abuse used NIMSS to initiate and fund violence prevention programs. Similarly, GFSA is currently using NIMSS data to justify and initiate gun-free zones in at least 25 schools in the three South African provinces of Gauteng, KwaZulu-Natal and the Western Cape.

Below we present a description of how injury data were utilized in the gun-free campaign and the Johannesburg Southern Metropolitan Council's decision to support the construction of a pedestrian bridge. We focus on specific contextual, content, process and social actor factors that enabled data uptake in each of these two case examples.

Factors That Influenced the Use of the Data in GFSA's Advocacy Campaign: Case Example 1

Contextual Factors

The first NIMSS reports were produced when there was a strong official re-emergence of a public health focus in South Africa and a fairly responsive political environment (Butchart, Hamber, Terre Blanche & Seedat, 1997). Even though GFSA had to contend with opposition from the pro-gun lobby and passive disengagement from minority political parties such as the New National Party (NNP), representatives of the majority party, the African National Congress (ANC), were very responsive to receiving information. In short, the NIMSS and its reports arose in a context of emerging democracy wherein there was special growing appreciation for the merits of scientifically produced data, the spirit of consultation, issue-based alliances, and democratic systems for informing and developing policy.

TABLE 1. Why and By Whom NIMSS Data Was Used

Use	Pathologists	NGOs	Govt. Departments	Universities
Education and Public Debate		✓	✓	
Policy Influence: Advocacy		✓	✓	
Informing Internal Policy: Management Tool	✓		✓	✓
Teaching, Training & Research	✓		✓	✓
Strengthening Commitments to Implement Legislation		✓	✓	
Building and Strengthening Cross-Sectorial Alliances		✓		
Justify New Projects & Lobbying for Intervention	✓	✓	✓	
Academic Presentations	✓	✓		✓
Media Presentations, including Internal Newsletters		✓		
Initiate Prevention Projects		✓	✓	
Further Funding/Funds	✓	✓	✓	

Content Factors

Gun-Free South Africa produced a Gun Control Charter, which detailed the nature of suggested reforms to the existing legislation. The Charter strengthened agreement on the need for stricter gun-control, highlighted priority areas needing advocacy action, and allowed alliance partners to support clauses that related to their respective core business without imposing a particular perspective. The 1999 annual mortality surveillance report detailed the manner of non-natural deaths, external causes of non-natural deaths, homicides, fatal accidents, and deaths arising from burns, falls and other unintentional incidents (e.g., drownings). The data accordingly provided an empirical support for the Charter.

Process Factors

Figure 2 captures the dynamically informed process that GFSA followed in its advocacy campaign for gun-control legislative reform. The process is not necessarily a linear one as many activities, such as information-sharing meetings with parliamentarians, occurred on an ongoing basis. The meetings with strategically placed parliamentarians and

FIGURE 2. Process in Advocating for Gun-Control Reforms: Gun-Free South Africa's Experience

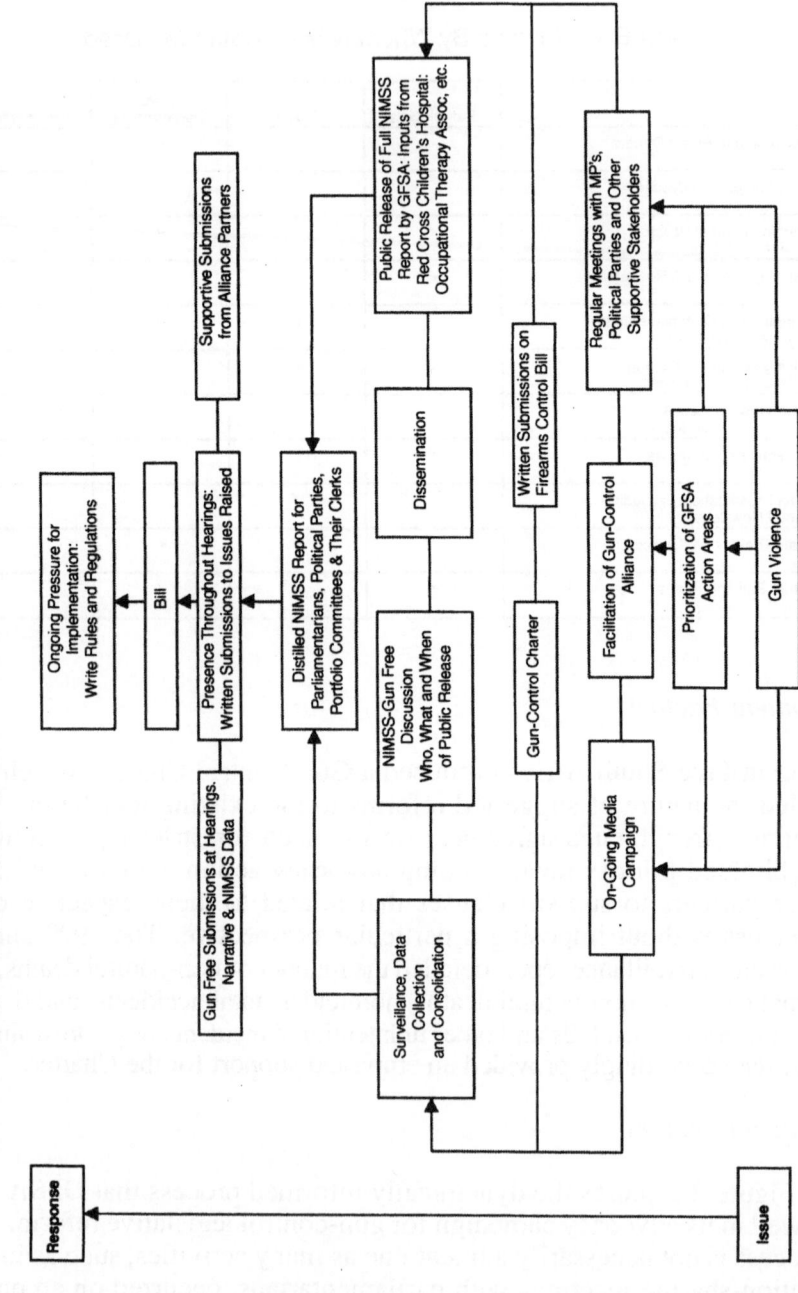

relevant portfolio committees, and the ongoing media campaign were designed to mobilize public and political support for the recommended gun-control reforms. The campaign gained impetus through the development of a Gun Control Charter and written submissions for consideration in the development of the Firearms Control Bill. Subsequently the full mortality surveillance report, collated and developed by the surveillance consortium, was released by GFSA at a public meeting to provide empirical muscle to its gun-control campaign. Through its daily presence at public hearings, GFSA was also able to respond to specific concerns through written submissions, and so defined itself as a resource that could be accessed beyond the specific gun-control legislative reform process.

Social Actors' Influences

Although the gun-control alliance and GFSA operated as significant social actors through the campaign, their spokesperson, Adele Kirsten, was projected as the key public face of the gun-control campaign. As a major social actor, Adele Kirsten articulated the interests and beliefs of the broad-based gun-control alliance. However, further research is required to understand how the actions and beliefs of other significant social actors such as members of the Safety and Security Portfolio Committee, and representatives of the Gun Lobby came to bear on the drafting and promulgation of the final bill which was endorsed by the South African Parliament in 2001.

In summary, the campaign process indicates that NIMSS generated data were significantly incorporated alongside other forms of information (e.g., narratives) to influence and inform the gun-legislative reforms. Even though the Gun Control Alliance was already established, the written submissions incorporating NIMSS data during the later stages of the campaign significantly strengthened the GFSA's recommendations and overall verbal submissions at the parliamentary hearings.

Factors That Influenced the Use of Epidemiological Data in Bridge Campaign: Case Example 2

Contextual Factors

The neighborhood safety promotion study report was produced during the reign of the first democratically elected local governments. Local authorities such as the SMLC, which housed many former health promotion activists familiar with the public health approach, formulated strategic alliances and plans, focused on measurable deliverables. In short, the neighborhood safety promotion study emerged in a context of localized political democracy wherein many local administrators and politicians were highly responsive to scientifically generated delivery in the health and social development sector.

Content Factors

The study report, presented in July 1997, profiled the injury magnitude and all the major injury types (e.g., violence, traffic, home injuries) and risk factors associated with these injury types (e.g., alcohol abuse, poverty), and prioritized violence prevention and traffic safety measures. In addition to calling for the stabilization and development of the neighborhoods, in the case of traffic injuries the researchers recommended environmental modifications to high-risk roads (e.g., the introduction of safe pedestrian crossing points, the installation of traffic lights, and the construction of pedestrian overhead bridges). Despite the complex issues associated with violence, the submission indicated that violence may be reduced through the regulation of alcohol sales, the installation of street lighting, appropriately targeted visible policing, and the promotion of peer support groups that could function to assist victims of intimate and acquaintance violence.

Following the formal acceptance and endorsement of the report by the SMLC, the construction of a pedestrian overhead bridge connecting the informal settlement of Slovo Park to the formal sectors of the larger Eldorado Park area was accorded priority.

Process Factors

Figure 3 below reveals that the process for informing local government traffic safety practice contained several stages that were not necessarily mutually exclusive. These stages included the preparation and presentation of a scientifically informed injury profile submission to local government and the participant community. This submission, together with the mobilisation of political and financial support from local political figures and health administrators, and community pressure, ultimately resulted in the construction of the pedestrian bridge. This case example is indicative of an instance when community pressure, political will, administrative support and institutional capacity merged with research inputs to introduce a specific traffic safety measure.

FIGURE 3. Process in SMLC Bridge Development

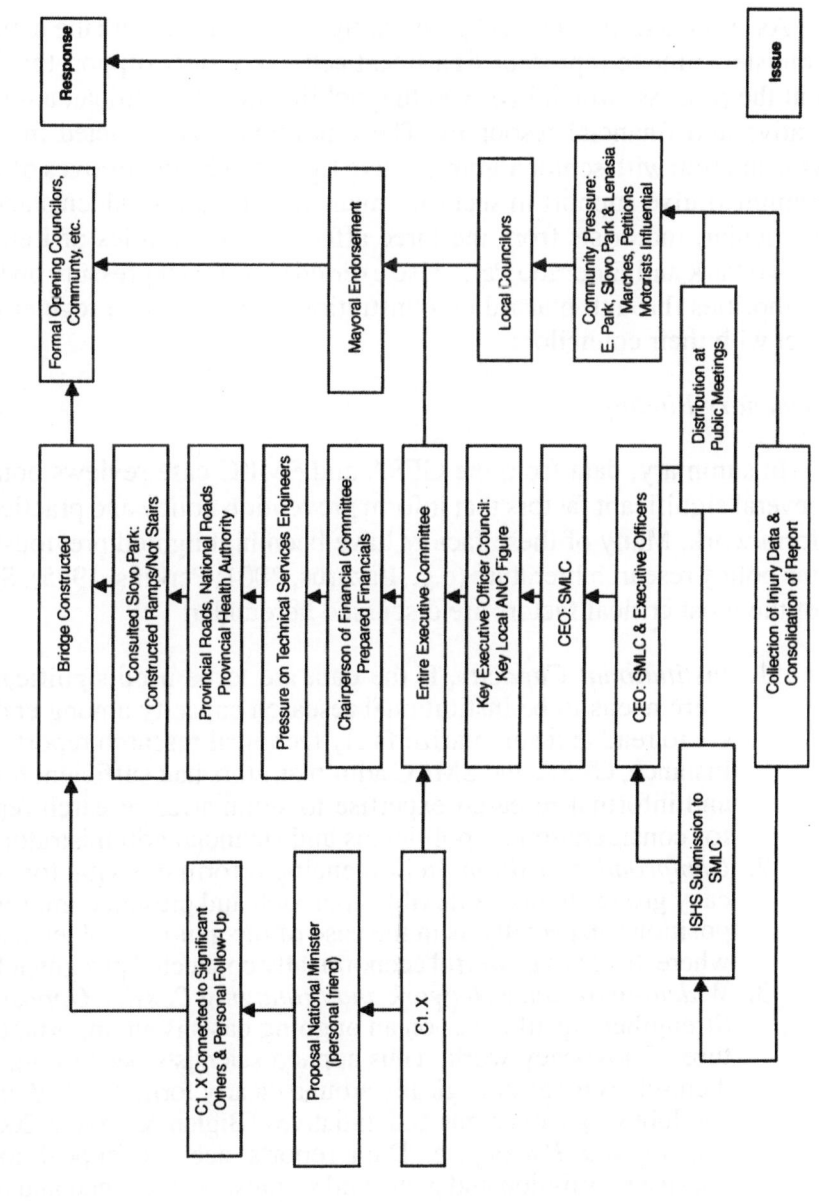

Social Actors' Influences

As alluded to above, local political figures in liaison with the national minister came to represent significant active political support throughout the process, which involved the mobilization of political, administrative and financial resources. These political figures acted in close consultation with senior administrative figures, who themselves offered administrative support in securing financial support. Residents and, in particular, motorists from the three affected communities of Lenasia, Slovo Park and Eldorado Park, also exerted significant pressure on local authorities through placard demonstrations, petitions and regular contact with their councilors.

Summary Findings

In summary, data from the GFSA and SMLC case reviews point to several significant factors that inform prevention policy and practice reform work. Many of these factors have been highlighted previously in the policy research literature (e.g., Lazarus, 2001; Perkins, 1995). Some of the most critical factors are discussed hereunder:

1. *Institutional Capacity.* If the data are to be used significantly, there needs to be institutional research capacity among end-users to read and summarize fairly technical research reports. For instance, GFSA and SMLC administrators had sufficient formal and informal research expertise to summarize research reports for consideration by politicians and financial administrators.
2. *Compromise Position.* In influencing reform it is vital for advocacy groups to take a flexible approach and present compromise positions, especially as in the case of the gun-control legislation where there is a powerful economically connected pro-gun lobby.
3. *Widening Alliance Network and Managing Passive Opposition.* Strengthening alliances on an ongoing basis is an important feature of advocacy work. Thus applied scientists need to organize themselves more strategically around clearly formulated advocacy and lobbying campaigns and initiatives (Biglan & Taylor, 2001).
4. *Appeal and Packaging.* Data reports need to appeal to the end-users' mission and goals and so must be packaged and regularly disseminated in friendly, accessible, non-jargonized documents (Biglan & Taylor, 2001).

5. *Timing*. The timing of data release is as significant as the data itself. Release during the festive season, for instance, is unlikely to generate public and political support.
6. *Personal Motivation and Connection to the Problem*. Involvement from key social actors who are strategically placed and familiar with problems, recommendations and data proved vital in both our case examples.
7. *Mounting Pressure from Affected Communities*. In the case of the pedestrian bridge, pressure from the affected communities and citizen participation were significant for mobilizing the requisite resources (Lazarus, 2001).
8. *Political Responsiveness*. Support from the dominant political party and its caucus is instrumental, as illustrated in the case of the bridge when the local councilor secured support from the local ANC branch.
9. *Institutional Reputation*. The reputation, standing and legitimacy of the research institution are as significant as the quality of data and associated reports.
10. *Multiple Sources of Influence*. Scientists represent only one of many powerful social groups seeking to influence policy and practice. The logic and rationality of social science and public health research may not always be shared or appreciated by decision-makers and other possible end-users. Thus, when scientifically produced data converge with the priorities of other social actors we note a significant impact on policy and practice, (Lazarus, 2001; Perkins, 1995).

CONCLUSION

Our findings suggest that the uptake of data is influenced by contextual factors (e.g., political receptivity to science), content factors (e.g., the structure and accessibility of scientifically informed reports), process factors (e.g., the timing of report submissions), and the interests of significant social actors.

While empirically produced data may be used constructively to inform policy formulation, development and implementation, sometimes end-users may well use data selectively to bolster their own position. We are therefore challenged to develop strategies to combat and minimize the misuse and misapplication of empirically generated data so as to maximize the utility of science within recently democratized societies such as South Africa.

REFERENCES

Biglan, A. & Taylor, T.K. (2000). Why have we been more successful in reducing tobacco use than violent crime? *American Journal of Community Psychology, 28*(3), 269-302.

Buehler, J.W. (1998). Surveillance. In K.J. Rothman & S. Greenland (Eds.), *Modern Epidemiology* (pp. 435-458). Second Edition. Philadelphia: Lippincott-Raven Publishers.

Burrows, S. (2001). The utility of surveillance data in mobilising injury prevention measures in South Africa. Unpublished manuscript. Johannesburg: Unisa Institute for Social and Health Sciences.

Butchart, A. (Ed.) (1999). *A profile of fatal injuries in South Africa 1999. First Annual Report of the National Injury Mortality Surveillance System.* Johannesburg: Unisa Institute for Social and Health Sciences.

Butchart, A., Hamber, B., Terre Blanche, M. & Seedat, M. (1997). Violence, power and mental health policy in twentieth century South Africa. In D. Foster, M. Freeman & Y. Pillay (Eds.), *Mental Health Policy Issues for South Africa* (pp. 236-262). Pretoria: MASA.

Butchart, A. & Kruger, J. (2001). Public health and community psychology: A case study in community-based injury prevention. In M. Seedat (Ed.), N. Duncan & S. Lazarus (Cons. Eds.), *Community Psychology: Theory, Method and Practice. South African and Other Perspectives* (pp. 215-241). Cape Town: Oxford University Press.

Declich, S. & Carter, A.O. (1994). Public health surveillance: Historical origins, methods and evaluation. *Bulletin of the World Health Organization, 72,* 285-304.

Gilson, L., Doherty, J., Mcintyre, D., Thomas, S., Brijlal, V., Bowa, C. & Mbatsha, S. (1999). *The dynamics of policy change: Health care financing in South Africa, 1994-1999.* Johannesburg: University of Witwatersrand.

Innes, D. (1997). Assessing the ANC's first three years in office. *The Innes Labour Brief, 8*(4), 7-20.

Jason, L.A. (1991). Participating in social change: A fundamental value of our discipline. *Journal of Community Psychology, 19*(1), 1-16.

Laflamme, L., Eilert-Petersen, E. & Schelp, L. (1999). Public health surveillance, injury prevention and safety promotion. In L. Laflamme, L. Svanström & L. Schelp (Eds.), *Safety Promotion Research: A Public Health Approach to Accident and Injury Prevention* (pp. 63-82). Stockholm: Karolinska Institutet.

Larkin, M. (1998). Global aspects of health and health policy in Third World Countries. In R. Kiely & P. Marfleet (Eds.), *Globalisation and the Third World* (pp. 91-112). London: Routledge.

Lazarus, S. (2001). Social policy and community psychology in South Africa. In M. Seedat (Ed.), N. Duncan and S. Lazarus (Cons. Eds.), *Community Psychology. Theory, Method and Practice. South African and Other Perspectives* (pp. 343-367). Cape Town: Oxford University Press.

Mercy, J.A., Ikeda, R. & Powell, K.E. (1998). Firearm-related injury surveillance: An overview of progress and the challenges ahead. *American Journal of Preventive Medicine, 15*(3), 6-16.

Nabudere, D.W. (2000). Globalisation, the African post-colonial state, post-tradition-alism, and the new world order. In D.W. Nabudere (Ed.), *Globalisation and the Post-Colonial African State* (pp. 11-55). Zimbabwe: AAPS Books.

Perkins, D.D. (1995). Speaking truth to power: Empowerment ideology as social inter-vention and policy. *American Journal of Community Psychology, 23*(5), 765-794.

Rickel, A. (1993). Congressional fellowship: Psychology's chance to influence health policy. *The Community Psychologist, 26*(3), 13.

Solarz, A.L. (1995). *Psychologists and public policy: What are we to do?* Paper pre-sented at the XXVth Inter-American Congress of Psychology, Puerto Rico.

Stack, L. & Ndletyana, M. (2001). *Understanding policy implementation: An explora-tion of research areas in the health sector.* Johannesburg: Centre for Policy Studies.

World Health Assembly (1996). *Prevention of violence: Public health priority.* Geneva: WHO (WHA 94,25).

World Health Organization (1999). *Injury: A leading cause of the global burden of dis-ease.* Geneva: WHO.

Women's Leadership Programs in South Africa: A Strategy for Community Intervention

Cheryl de la Rey
Gia Jankelowitz

University of Cape Town

Shahaaz Suffla

University of South Africa

SUMMARY. A central premise of this paper is that the training of women for leadership roles is a critical component of the development of communities as a whole. This was the central point of departure for a study that aimed to review women's leadership training programs in South Africa. This paper reports on this study in which 38 organizations

Cheryl de la Rey is currently editor of the *South African Journal of Psychology* and Associate Professor at the University of Cape Town. Her research interests are community and peace psychology with a focus on gender and race.

Gia Jankelowitz worked on this project as part of her graduate studies in Psychology at the University of Cape Town.

Shahaaz Suffla's professional work is in clinical psychology. Her research focus is on women and safety prevention in communities.

Address correspondence to: Cheryl de la Rey (Associate Professor), Bremner Building, Room 202, University of Cape Town, Private Bag, Rondebosch 7701, Cape Town, South Africa (E-mail: DeLaReyC@BREMNER.uct.ac.za) (C. de la Rey).

[Haworth co-indexing entry note]: "Women's Leadership Programs in South Africa: A Strategy for Community Intervention." de la Rey, Cheryl, Gia Jankelowitz, and Shahaaz Suffla. Co-published simultaneously in *Journal of Prevention & Intervention in the Community* (The Haworth Press, Inc.) Vol. 25, No. 1, 2003, pp. 49-64; and: *Prevention and Intervention Practice in Post-Apartheid South Africa* (ed: Vijé Franchi; cons. ed: Norman Duncan) The Haworth Press, Inc., 2003, pp. 49-64.

from across the country participated. Three main data sources were used: Organizational materials, interviews and questionnaires. The analysis examined the following key features: Motivation for leadership training, approaches to leadership, understandings of gender difference, training techniques and strategies and outcomes. The findings revealed trends that may have implications for best practice frameworks in interventions targeted at leadership, gender and development. *[Article copies available for a fee from The Haworth Document Delivery Service: 1-800-HAWORTH. E-mail address: <docdelivery@haworthpress.com> Website: <http://www. HaworthPress.com> © 2003 by The Haworth Press, Inc. All rights reserved.]*

KEYWORDS. Women's leadership training programs, gender and development, community intervention, South Africa

INTRODUCTION

Internationally, reports emphasize that despite the dramatic increase of women in the work force, women are still under-represented in positions of power, responsibility and leadership (Stanford & Oates, 1995). This trend is evident in South Africa despite some increases in the number of women leaders in the post-apartheid era. For example, the number of women occupying parliamentary and governmental positions in South Africa increased from 28% in 1994 to 30% in the 1998 elections (Gender Advocacy Program, 2000). But this percentage is still small in comparison to men and the percentage of women leaders at community levels is much smaller. There are many women who are committed and eager to enter these community leadership positions but their under-developed skills undermine their capacity to do so.

Leadership training programs (LTPs) can be extremely effective in improving or developing an individual's leadership abilities (Laird, 1985; Mitchiner, 2000; Stodgill, 1974). The enhancement of leadership may then lead to growth and increased productivity in an organization (Mitchiner, 2000). Training may be defined as an experience that causes individuals to acquire new leadership skills or enhance their previous leadership behavior (Laird, 1985).

In South Africa a range of women's LTPs exist, yet there is no clarity regarding target participants, training content, evaluation strategies, underlying assumptions, and potential effectiveness. This study aimed to review women's LTPs in South Africa. The findings provide a picture of the activities presently being undertaken by some organizations in

South Africa, which aim to increase women's leadership skills, and encourage women to occupy more leadership positions. The analysis identified implications for best practice frameworks and future policies.

THEORETICAL ISSUES

The trait theory of leadership claims that leaders possess certain traits or characteristics that contribute towards being an effective leader. Briefly, these traits include: effective communication, task completion, responsibility, problem solving, originality, decision-making, passion, vision, ethics, humor, embracing diversity, self-awareness, confidence, courage, experience and power (Foster, 2000; James, 1998; Karstan, 1994; Koestenbaum, 1991; Nadler & Tushmen, 1994; Stogdill, 1974; Whitten, 2000; Withers, 2000). Although in earlier writings 'traits' were regarded as inherent, theorists presently maintain that these traits may be learned (Mitchiner, 2000). LTPs are based on the premise that leadership can be taught and learned, and include activities that are designed to 'teach' the participants the above traits. Researchers claim that effective leadership training can enable anyone to become a leader (Foster, 2000; Hughes, Ginnett & Curphey, 1993; Mitchiner, 2000; Steven, 2000; Whitten, 2000).

There is ongoing debate on whether women have different leadership styles and traits than men (Eagly & Johnson, 1990; Powell, 1990). The one school of thought advocates that female leaders are not different from male leaders. This school proposes that women who pursue the non-traditional career of a leader reject the feminine stereotypes and have needs and styles similar to those of male leaders. Leaders in an organization are socialized and selected into their organizational role, which overrides their gender role. This results in little difference between male and female leaders (Korabik et al., 1993; Kushnell & Newton, 1986; Powell, 1990).

The other school proposes that women do have different leadership styles than male leaders. Eagly and Johnson (1990) in their meta-analyses on women and leadership found significant evidence for differences in leadership styles. They concluded that women adopted a more democratic or participative style while men adopted a more autocratic or directive style.

This difference perspective proposes that women possess unique leadership traits, and organizations and communities would benefit immensely from selecting and promoting women to higher leadership positions. Rosener (1990) reports that presently a second wave of women leaders are making their way into the top leadership positions by drawing on the unique skills and attitudes that they have developed through their socialization and from sharing their experiences. These women leaders are demonstrating that women can achieve successful results, but may take a different path.

Foster (2000) and James (1998) note that women's leadership positions have been hindered by discrimination and stereotyping. Overcoming these difficult circumstances has resulted in women developing a more co-operative and flexible model of leadership. Women leaders are breaking new ground and are eager to find ways to engage other disenfranchised communities, such as youth and ethnic minorities. Helgesen (1990) recognized that certain feminine characteristics give women leaders an advantage. These include heightened communication and interpersonal skills, conflict resolution skills, and a greater capacity for prioritizing than their male counterparts. Helgesen (1990) suggests that these traits may stem from managing a household and raising children, while at the same time juggling a career. Rosener (1990) found that women leaders were characterized by a style of interactive, 'transformational' leadership. They actively sought affirmative interactions with their subordinates and the creation of a work environment where everyone was involved. This reflects the woman leader's belief that the creation of a win-win situation is advantageous to the organization's production. Organizations in recent years have been criticized for their hierarchical and bureaucratic structure. Many organizations have started to adopt a flatter organizational structure, where interpersonal and participatory skills are required. Thus, women's dynamic leadership traits are ideal (Fierman, 1990; James, 1998; Helgesen, 1990; Moskal, 1997; Stanford & Oates, 1995).

Researchers question the effectiveness of women-only versus mixed gender LTPs. Women-only LTPs are advantageous as they provide a safe space for women leaders to address and tackle the issues they face, and develop more skills in certain areas. Women-only LTPs generally include modules on personal development and career planning, assertiveness skills and organizational change strategies. Women aiming for leadership positions generally lack self-confidence, and thus women-only LTPs provide the affirmation boost that most women leaders require. This increases their motivation and self-assurance (Bhavnani, 1997; Burke, 2000; Steven, 2000).

On the other end of the continuum, individuals believe that women-only LTPs exacerbate the gendered leadership problem and contribute to the stereotypical idea that women are unsuccessful and ineffective leaders. This perspective proposes that the implementation of mixed gender LTPs is of greater value. Mixed gender programs aim to deter bias against women and help dispel sex role stereotypes that exist in the organizations and communities. Women and men participants are encouraged to listen to one another and build authentic and significant relationships with one another. This results in participants feeling empowered, realizing the value of learning from one another, building relationships, and encourages the organization to work together interdependently and successfully (Betters-Reed & Moore, 1992).

METHOD

Data Collection

Three data sources were used, namely, organizational materials, interviews and questionnaires. These different sources were utilized so as to illuminate multiple perspectives and contribute to a richer data set (Tindall, 1994). The data collection was conducted using a phased approach beginning with interviews that informed the design of the questionnaire, which was subsequently distributed. Organizational materials were obtained during the interviews and were also submitted with the questionnaires.

A combination of convenience and purposive sampling was used. Twelve interviewees were selected because they represented a diversity of training and women's organizations, and conducted women's LTPs in different sectors. The interviewees were also selected on the basis of accessibility to the researcher. The semi-structured interviews lasted approximately 45-60 minutes, and were audio-taped with the permission of the interviewees. The interviewees were guaranteed anonymity. Structured topics included the aim, content, and the underlying assumptions of their program. Space was provided for free-flowing comments from the interviewees about training, views on women's leadership and future goals.

After reviewing the literature on women's leadership and training programs, a questionnaire was constructed. The interviews not only provided in-depth qualitative data, but also served the purpose of piloting the questionnaire. The questionnaire was revised accordingly. There is no clarity on the actual number of organizations that offer women's LTPs in South Africa, nor is there a comprehensive database. Therefore, questionnaires were distributed to as many organizations as possible that indicated some leadership training. Four hundred questionnaires were distributed nationally via facsimile and e-mail to all organizations named in various resource lists. The questionnaires aimed to provide an overview of the different women's LTPs presently active in South Africa. The questionnaire consisted of both fixed and open-ended questions. Questions were grouped into five categories, aimed at assessing the program's target audience, rationale and aims, training content and learning strategies, evaluation and assessment strategies, and underlying assumptions.

Twenty-six questionnaires were returned, yielding a response rate of 5.9%. In each case the respondent was the person directly responsible for the training program. Together with the interviewees' twelve organizations, this yielded a total sample of 38 organizations. All organizations also submitted information materials such as brochures and pamphlets.

Data Analysis

The twelve interviews were transcribed, and a thematic analysis was conducted using a coding framework that emanated from the data content. Initially the transcripts were read closely to identify units of meaning that were coded. These codes were then merged into categories and finally into themes of meaning. Frequency counts were derived from the questionnaire data. Organizational materials were read and themes were identified.

FINDINGS AND DISCUSSION

The themes extracted from the data are presented below beginning with a description of the final sample. Each theme is discussed in relation to the literature, noting points of confirmation and difference.

Sample Profile

To obtain a profile of this sample, data from the 12 interviews and the 26 questionnaire responses were combined (n = 38). The percentage of organizations aimed directly at women was 44% (17). Of the organizations not directly aimed at women, i.e., 55% (21), 47% (10) reported a 70-90% female attendance of their LTPs, and 19% (4) indicated about 80% female attendance. Only 33% (7) indicated less than 50% female attendance.

Target Groups and Context

Organizations in this sample reported adjusting their programs to meet the needs of the different communities in South Africa. For example, courses would be changed to accommodate language differences. The percentage of organizations that indicated that they conducted the programs in English was 95% (36), in Afrikaans 47% (18) and in an African language 53% (20).[1] Most of the organizations reported that their programs are conducted in multiple, parallel languages where the facilitators are multilingual or work through an interpreter, or the workshop participants translate for each other.

The literature on LTPs, which tends to focus on management and training conducted in large corporations, was often inapplicable to the South African context, where programs are adapted for a range of target audiences. The results indicate that most of the organizations target more than one audience, i.e., rural 74% (28), urban 61% (23) and peri-urban 63% (24) communities, and 82% (31) of the organizations report targeting all races. The programs are required to adapt their content for the diverse sectors. The percentage of participating organizations that reported targeting skilled workers was 68% (26) and those targeting unskilled workers was 50% (19). A majority of the respondents emphasized the value of the programs being conducted in a community setting, with 47% (18) reporting that they conduct their program in the community, and 37% (14) of the organizations stating that they conduct the program at their offices. The reported advantages of conducting the program in the community included a greater feeling of familiarity for participants, increased sensitivity to the cultural context, and greater chance of success and sustainability.

Payment for Training

Mixed responses were reported on the issue of participants paying for the course themselves. Forty-two percent (16) of the organizations reported that participants are sponsored and do not pay for the course themselves. One interviewee strongly advocated that, "We've seen that the people who pay for themselves or are paid for by their family or who have a vested interest in the program, tend to take it more seriously," and another commented, "When they pay, value is given to the course." These comments illustrate one of the reasons why 37% (14) of the organizations reported that the participants pay for the course themselves. One organization sponsors their rural participants entirely, but promotes 'sweat equity' where the participants collect money for food, and where they need to do their work in order to obtain the course certificate. When asked if the program was sponsored, 47% (18) of the respondents reported yes, 8% (3) reported no, 42% (16) reported partially. Reflecting the South African financial situation, many of the respondents reported difficulty in obtaining outside funding and sponsorship.

Motivation for Leadership Training

Many of the LTPs in this sample target individuals already identified as leaders in their community. As a result, the programs aim to enhance the participant's leadership potential and provide the skills for them to reach their full capacity with the objective of achieving community upliftment and sustainability. The responses to an open-ended question to state the aim of their LTP included key words, such as 'team leadership' and 'community organizing.' These aims resonate with the literature, which emphasizes that in addition to viewing a leader as an individual, it is essential to recognize that the community participates in the leadership process and that the leader should aim to positively influence the community towards an accomplished goal.

Empowerment

The word 'empowerment' surfaced numerous times in the interviews when explaining the aims of programs. The definitions of empowerment varied, yet a common thread was that individuals must first empower themselves before they can empower the community. The following definition of empowerment is an example:

> Empowerment, it's when they never had opportunities but we created opportunities for them to do certain things. It's one, using their capacities. It's two, the education. They are empowered to work on a plan for the project, empowered to work on project goals and objectives, so you empower them to do those certain things.

The interviewees' definitions of empowerment strongly resonate with Wallerstein's (1992, as cited in Wolfe, Wekerle & Scott, 1997) definition. He proposes that empowerment involves people gaining control and mastery over their own lives. Empowerment implies change and social action, where people, organizations and communities are encouraged to work towards a common goal and the improved quality of community life.

Defining Leadership

The personality characteristics and behavior traits associated with leadership were (n = 26): 'participatory' (77%, 20), 'person-orientated' (73%, 19), 'interpersonal' (85%, 22), and 'vision' (81%, 21). This 'participatory' definition of leadership underlies the programs' activities. An illustrative example is:

> A leader needs to be receptive to people, a leader needs to be the one that listens to people, and the leader is the one that is being directed by the vision of the people. A leader to me is the one that is working with communities, but also creating a space for participation in the community, identifying a problem and then outlining for the community, and then the community participating and supporting that person.

Gender and Leadership

The literature overview highlighted the perspective that advocated the existence and characteristics of a feminine style of leadership (Fierman, 1990; Rosener, 1990; Stanford & Oates, 1995). This perspective emanated in the data. Most of the respondents reported that men and women differ in leadership styles. In comparison to men, women leaders were described as having better interpersonal skills, being more sensitive, caring, democratic, flexible and more encouraging of participation.

These findings support Stanford and Oates' (1995) heuristic model of female leadership, which points out that women leaders are characterized as participative. One of the interviewees explained:

> The difference between female and male leadership to me, is the ability to walk in the shoes of the follower, to understand the needs of the follower, and to really only stay one or two steps ahead, and not run away from the follower, not get behind them . . . women leaders that we work with are most definitely, spiritually more intelligent.

Training Techniques and Strategies

Block Modules

Lambert (1994) emphasizes that LTPs should be conducted in block modules, as repeated interaction creates a greater opportunity to influence behavior and establish informal networks. In this study, 77% (20) of the organizations reported that their programs are conducted in the form of modules. All the interviewees emphasized that as a result of the short attention span and pressured schedules of adult participants, a modular program is effective. In the period between modules participants are assigned activities to implement in their community. This results in participants returning for the next module, having already put the acquired skills into practice. They are able to report on the effectiveness of their performance and ask advice for improvement. In summary, the benefit of a modular program is that it enables ongoing monitoring, testing and evaluation.

Participatory Learning

The questionnaire asked the respondents to select the factors that would best describe the features of the learning design used in their LTP. The most frequently identified factors were participative style (92%, 24), experiential activities (88%, 23), and questioning style (88%, 23). This finding was supported by the interviewees, who described their programs as implementing participatory action learning methods with an emphasis on group interaction and experiential learning. An example of the implementation and advantages of a participatory learning style is the following description by one of the interviewees of her activities with rural women:

> What I try to do, is make it as participatory as possible, with as little amount of lecturing as possible, because lecturing goes in one ear and out the other, especially for people who have not had much formal education, then participatory education is better. I try to keep it very practical and very realistic, and not really on the theory.

Numerous aspects were incorporated into the sub-theme of participatory learning style. The style of the instructors was described as facilitative (85%, 22) rather than authoritarian (4%, 1). Another aspect of a participatory learning style related to the use of multiple learning methods and training aids. The interviewees mentioned the use of case studies, manuals, videos, role-plays and billboards. These methods aim to encourage the participants to be actively involved in the learning process. This was supported in the questionnaire, where many advocated a 'doing style' (77%, 20) rather than a 'telling style' (23%, 6).

These findings echo Wallerstein's (1992, as cited in Wolfe et al., 1997) empowerment education model, which is based on the principle that participation is the active agent in empowerment. He maintains that programs must incorporate activities that actively involve the participants as "co-investigators," and participants are encouraged to explore issues and develop strategies that may positively transform the community.

Networking

Networking is a strategy that helps women achieve greater leadership positions (Karstan, 1994; Rosen, Miguel & Pierce, 1994). Twenty-one (81%) interviewees reported that networking is an important skill that they impart and implement in their LTPs. This is achieved through using facilitators from other organizations, creating a database of participants and sending out newsletters to alert the participants as to what aid is available and what activities are being conducted. As expressed by one of the interviewees:

> We find that women are talking about going up the ladder, but we're not talking about going up the ladder we're talking about a cobweb, whereby people can go anyway and anyhow and that would be that you have a network, and if you fall you have a place to fall on; a safety net.

Creative Evaluation Approaches

Evaluation is pertinent to any LTP design. Self-evaluation ensures that the learners have gained from the program, and program evaluation indicates to the facilitators if the program was effective in achieving its desired objective (Hughes et al., 1993; Lambert, 1994; Laird, 1985).

The use of discussion to evaluate the program was reported more frequently (73%, 19) than the use of written questionnaires (50%, 13). Some of the interviewees claimed that a written evaluation of the program was not beneficial, as the participants fear writing negative comments. One interviewee noted that she calls the evaluation sheet a "smiley sheet." Numerous measures have been undertaken by the interviewees to avoid this problem. Instead of handing out the evaluation forms only once, some require the participants to fill out an evaluation form every day, which includes self-reflective questions, such as, "What did you learn?" This ongoing evaluation is advantageous as the program is improved daily, rather than receiving the evaluation at the end of the LTP.

Follow-Up and On-Site Visits

The interviewees stated that although they use evaluation forms, the "real evaluation" of the programs' effectiveness is to examine if the participants are implementing their newly learned skills in the community. The only way this can be achieved is by having contact with the participants after the program and/or conducting a follow-up program. The questionnaire respondents all mentioned that they had contact with the participants after the program. The type of contact reported included monthly meetings, newsletters, e-mail correspondence and regular supervision.

All the interviewees indicated that follow-up in the form of on-site visits is essential, and advantageous. Interviewees reported that on-site visits provide an indication that the participants are actively implementing their newly learned skills, allow the program developers to gauge the impact of the program in the community context, show support and commitment to the participants, provide an effective program evaluation method and indicate areas of improvement. Yet, only a few of the interviewees said that they conducted on-site visits because of a lack of sufficient finances and sponsorship.

Women-Only or Mixed Gender Training

As mentioned previously, there is debate about which LTPs are more beneficial: women-only or mixed gender LTP programs. Most of the interviewees mentioned that there is a market for women-only LTPs. The interviewees acknowledged that women lack self-confidence and doubt their leadership abilities. Women-only LTPs were seen to alleviate these problems, as they provide a safe space for women, build the women's confidence by providing assurance and affirmation, and acknowledge that women have the ability to become powerful leaders in their community (Bhavnani, 1997; Steven, 2000).

The interviewees implementing women-only LTPs highlighted that these programs create a space for participants to discuss important issues that specifically affect women. These issues include, amongst others: child care, gender discrimination, balancing work and family, managing stress, sexual harassment, AIDS counseling, the 'pull-her-down' syndrome and the 'queen-bee' syndrome. Some interviewees mentioned that women-only LTPs allow the facilitator and participants to discuss techniques of how to lead in a traditionally male dominated leadership space, and encourage women leaders to create their own space. The following is illustrative:

> Women will find it safer, more comfortable, and will be freer to express ideas. Same way looking at girls' schools, free to develop in maths and science. Girls develop freely when competition of men is removed . . . experiencing who they are, not fearing challenge, not being indoctrinated.

In spite of the support for women-only LTPs, this was not seen as a method that should be continued into the future by 73% (19). Two main reasons emerged as to why mixed gender LTP should be implemented. The first reason suggests that mixed gender LTPs promote the acceptance of differences and diversity, and encourage men and women to learn about and support each other. Respondents reported that women-only LTPs, through the exclusion of men, create greater alienation. Mixed gender LTPs were viewed as representing real life dynamics. One of the questionnaire respondents highlighted the value of mixed gender LTPs by reporting that, "I think the challenge is to be able to lead no matter whether we are different in gender or race." This echoes Betters-Reeds and Moore (1992), who promote diversity training as beneficial in removing stereotypes and empowering individuals.

The second reason reported by respondents is that mixed gender LTPs provide a space to educate and shift the attitudes of men. These comments demonstrated that the advantages of conducting mixed gender LTPs are that they "force men to examine their sexist attitudes," "challenge patriarchal assumption of power and dominance," and that they encourage men to "learn how to work positively with women." Respondents reported that mixed gender LTPs are extremely beneficial in encouraging men to eradicate their stereotypical belief that a leader is male, and instead to learn to accept women as competent and valuable leaders.

Standardization and Accreditation

Many of the interviewees recommended external accreditation for the programs. This issue was stressed as pertinent to South Africa, where a large percentage of individuals were unable to obtain an education due to the past political system of apartheid. The following response was typical:

There are so many programs, so much bogus stuff going on in this
country and people issuing bogus certificates, and people paying
through the nose for them, and at the end of the day they are actu-
ally competent in nothing. . . . There is so much of this.

Many of the interviewees proposed that one way to alleviate this type
of problem is to establish an external organization to accredit worthy
programs. They believed that this would result in a standardization of
programs, and participants would receive credits that render them eligi-
ble to attend a higher institution of learning. The comments mentioned
in the open-question section of the questionnaires indicated the advantages of implementing an external standardization board. These included ensuring that training organizations meet the standards set for
the quality and content of programs, creating a monitoring system that
ensures greater accountability and transparency, and ensuring that the
proposed quality of the service is being delivered.

CONCLUSION

Through an analysis of LTPs, this study investigated activities that os-
tensibly seek to increase the number of women community leaders in
South Africa by training women in skills needed to occupy leadership positions. The findings revealed clear trends that may inform work towards
the identification of a best practice framework for women's leadership
training. In sum, experiential, participatory methods were deemed most
suitable. Furthermore, to accommodate the multiple demands on women,
training should be organized in block modules. The need for follow-up
monitoring and evaluation was considered critical, but not always feasi-
ble due to resource limitations. Accreditation of courses was seen as desirable, specifically for the purpose of quality assurance.

NOTE

1. Most of the questions in the questionnaire asked the respondents to select the options that applied. This resulted in more than one option being selected (maximum =
26). In order to obtain the sample profile, the 12 interviews and 36 questionnaire responses were combined, and frequency counts were converted into percentages by dividing the total number of questionnaires and interviews completed by (n = 38). In the
rest of the article, percentages are obtained for the questionnaire respondents only, by
dividing the frequency counts (n = 26). This illustrates the percentage of subjects/orga-
nizations that agreed with a particular option presented. Percentages are rounded off.

REFERENCES

Betters-Reed, B.L. and Moore, L.L. (1992). Managing diversity: Focusing on women and the whitewash dilemma. In U. Sekaran, and F.T.L. Leong (Eds.), *Womenpower: Managing in Times of Demographic Turbulence* (pp.31-58). London: Sage Publications.

Bhavnani, R. (1997). Personal development and women's training: Transforming the agenda. *Women in Management Review, 12*(4), 140-49.

Burke, R. (2000). Do managerial men benefit from organizational values supporting work-personal life balance? *Women in Management Review, 15*(1), 81-89.

Eagly, A.H. and Johnson, B.T. (1990). Gender and leadership style: A meta-analysis. *Psychological Bulletin, 108*(2), 233-256.

Fierman, J. (1990). Do women manage differently? *Fortune, 17,* 71-74.

Foster, R. (2000). Leadership in the twenty-first century: Working to build a civil society. *National Civic Review, 89*(1), 87-93.

Gender Advocacy Program (2000). *Women in Parliament Directory, Gender Advocacy Program,* Cape Town.

Helgesen, S. (1990). *The Female Advantage: Women's Ways of Leadership.* New York: Doubleday.

Hughes, R.L., Ginnett, R.C. and Curphy, G.J. (1993). *Leadership: Enhancing the Lessons of Experience.* Sydney, Australia: Richard D. Irwin, Inc.

James, A. (1998). Mary, Mary quite contrary, how do women leaders grow? *Women in Management Review, 13*(2), 67-71.

Karstan, M.F. (1994). *Management and Gender: Issues and Attitudes.* Westport, Connecticut: Praeger Publishers.

Koestenbaum, P. (1991). *Leadership: The Inner Side of Greatness.* San Francisco: Jossey-Bass Publishers.

Korabik, K., Baril, G.L. and Watson, C. (1993). Managers' conflict management style and leadership effectiveness: The moderating effects of gender. *Sex Roles, 29,* 405-420.

Kushnell, E. and Newton, R. (1986). Gender, leadership style, and subordinate satisfaction: An experiment. *Sex Roles, 14,* 203-208.

Laird, D. (1985). *Approaches to Training and Development* (2nd ed.). California: Addison-Wesley Publishing Company Inc.

Lambert, L.L. (1994). Nine reasons that most training programs fail. In C.E. Schneier, C.J. Russell, R.W. Beatty, and L.S. Baird (Eds.), *The Training and Development Sourcebook* (pp. 45-48). Amherst, Massachusetts: Human Resource Development Press.

Mitchiner, M. (2000). Leadership skills: The overlooked training. *South Carolina Business Journal, 19*(1), 10-12.

Moskal, B.S. (1997). Women make better managers. *Industry Week, 246*(3), 17-19.

Nadler, D.A. and Tushmen, M.L. (1994). Beyond the charismatic leader: Leadership and organizational change. In C.E. Schneier, C.J. Russell, R.W. Beatty, and L.S. Baird (Eds.), *The Training and Development Sourcebook* (pp. 278-292). Amherst, Massachusetts: Human Resource Development Press.

Powell, G. (1990). One more time: Do female and male managers differ? *Academy of Management Executive, 4*(3), 68-75.

Rosen, B., Miguel, M. and Pierce, E. (1994). Stemming the exodus of women managers. In C.E. Schneier, C.J. Russell, R.W. Beatty, and L.S. Baird (Eds.), *The Training and Development Sourcebook* (pp. 350-360). Amherst, Massachusetts: Human Resource Development Press.

Rosener, J.D. (1990). Ways women lead. *Harvard Business Review, 68*, 119-124.

Stanford, J. H. and Oates, B.R. (1995). Women's leadership styles: A heuristic analysis. *Women in Management Review, 10*(2), 9-17.

Steven, V. (2000). A stairway to the stars for 'unskilled' women. *Women in Management Review, 15*(1/2), 20-32.

Stogdill, R.M. (1974). *Handbook of Leadership: A Survey of Theory and Research.* New York: The Free Press.

Tindall, C. (1994). Issues of evaluation. In P. Banister, E. Burman, I. Parker, M. Taylor, and C. Tindall (Eds.), *Qualitative Methods in Psychology: A Research Guide.* Buckingham: Open University Press.

Whitten, C. (2000). The value of leadership training. *Public Relations Tactics, 7*(2), 24-26.

Withers, P. (2000). Birth of a leader. *BC Business, 28*(1), 20-28.

Wolfe, D.A. Wekerle, C. & Scott, K. (1997). *Alternatives to Violence: Empowering Youth to Develop Healthy Relationships.* London: Sage.

Intervening in Communities at Multiple Levels: Combining Curative and Preventive Interventions

Anthony V. Naidoo

Sherine Van Wyk

University of Stellenbosch

SUMMARY. The Jamestown Community Project (JCP) evolved in response to a request for psychological services at the primary health clinic. This article describes the genesis, implementation and evaluation

Anthony V. Naidoo obtained his MA and PhD in Psychology at Ball State University, USA. He is professor in community psychology at the University of Stellenbosch, with a strong interest in translating and applying psychological theory and praxis in oppressed and disadvantaged community contexts. His areas of interest also extend to the career development of marginalized groups, group therapy and process, and eco-psychology.

Sherine Van Wyk is lecturer in psychology at the University of Stellenbosch. Her expertise is mainly in the area of mental health within the South African context. She has a keen interest in community and social issues with a focus on preventative measures.

Address correspondence to: Professor Anthony V. Naidoo, Department of Psychology, University of Stellenbosch, Private Bag X1, Matieland 7602, South Africa (E-mail: avnaidoo@ maties.sun.ac.za) (A.V. Naidoo).

The authors acknowledge the individual endeavors of the community role players, mentors and mentees, whose collective energies and aspirations constitute the Jamestown Community Project.

[Haworth co-indexing entry note]: "Intervening in Communities at Multiple Levels: Combining Curative and Preventive Interventions." Naidoo, Anthony V., and Sherine Van Wyk. Co-published simultaneously in *Journal of Prevention & Intervention in the Community* (The Haworth Press, Inc.) Vol. 25, No. 1, 2003, pp. 65-80; and: *Prevention and Intervention Practice in Post-Apartheid South Africa* (ed: Vijé Franchi: cons. ed: Norman Duncan) The Haworth Press, Inc., 2003, pp. 65-80.

of the project. Using a conceptual model of mental health intervention, we present the development of the JCP against the backdrop of several overlapping and inclusive conceptual and theoretical frameworks, namely the community psychology paradigm, program evaluation, action research and prevention. We foreground how the project has attempted to combine curative and preventive interventions serving the ideals of distributive equality and sufficiency, to operationalize concepts of partnership, empowerment, and participation at grassroots level. *[Article copies available for a fee from The Haworth Document Delivery Service: 1-800-HAWORTH. E-mail address: <docdelivery@haworthpress.com> Website: <http://www.HaworthPress.com> © 2003 by The Haworth Press, Inc. All rights reserved.]*

KEYWORDS. Mental health intervention, community psychology, program evaluation, action research, prevention

INTRODUCTION

The manner in which community problems are conceptualized and interpreted is likely to frame the types of solutions or interventions proposed to resolve them. In espousing the importance of an ecological perspective, Gregory Bateson (1972) asserts that it is the *context* that provides meaning to behavior, the interpretive canvas against which individual and collective behavior can be better understood. This is to some degree a reformulation of Lewin's classic equation $B = f(P,E)$ (quoted in Orford, 1992), where behavior is "the function of the person, the environment, and the interaction between the two" (p. 5). In a similar vein, Bronfenbrenner (1979) construes developmental behavior as being embedded within a social context shaped by micro-, meso-, exo- and macrosystem influences. These system influences are nested, interdependent, reciprocal in nature, integral to understanding human behavior, and should inform any intervention program.

In reviewing the politics of problem definition, Scileppi, Teed, and Torres (2000) argue that social problems are not viewed unilaterally by all, including mental health practitioners. Diverse constituencies have opposing vested interests in how a community problem is conceptualized and approached, and these groups often advocate for opposing solutions. Deciding who can frame the problem is an important first step in determining which approach to take to resolve it. Mental health professionals, unfortunately, are inclined to interpret their role narrowly, opting to provide individual oriented psychological services for community needs. While, in some instances, this approach has merit, it might be more beneficial for the community for other levels of intervention also to be considered (Scileppi et al., 2000). A contextual analysis of the problem may lead to a broader understanding of the problem, and different, more effective levels and types of intervention (Naidoo, Shabalala, & Bawa, in press). Hence, community psychology advocates moving beyond individual psychological difficulties, not only in thinking about higher levels of causation and influence but also in trying to bring about changes at these levels (Orford, 1992).

Reviews of the efficacy of preventive initiatives suggest that prevention programs are effective and enhanced when these are comprehensive, target multiple ecological levels and utilize combined approaches that facilitate enhancement/promotion and prevention/risk reduction (Felner, Felner, & Silverman, 2000). Prevention should be conceptualized to provide effective solutions to complex social problems and overcome the inefficient victim-blaming models that frequently reduce negative structural socio-political conditions to intra-psychic pathologies (Albee, 1982, 1986; Felner et al., 2000; Hook, 2002).

In South Africa, the provision of mental health services has been characterized by a western conceptual framework and overwhelming racialised inequalities (Lazarus, 1988). For decades the mental health profession has focused its energies and resources primarily on the individual as target and on remedial and curative intervention goals. This traditional focus has served the needs of only a small section of the South African population, limiting the availability and accessibility of mental health services for the majority of the population (Freeman, 1990; Pillay & Petersen, 1996; Seedat, Duncan & Lazarus, 2001). Furthermore, the concentration of psychologists and psychological services in urban areas and the deprivation of rural and township communities of mental health services warrant urgent attention and compound the need for redress and equity (Freeman, 1990; Pillay & Petersen, 1996). The World Health Organization (WHO) Report (2001) draws attention to the finding that globally mental health has essentially been neglected or ignored, suggesting that governments should formulate and implement policies to ensure the promotion of the mental health of their citizens. It regards the integration of mental health services into the public health system as a more successful proven approach (WHO, 2001). The Department of Health in its Health Sector Strategic Framework 1999-2004 (2002) has declared primary and community-based health care as its primary objective, focusing on an efficient, preventive and promotive health care system. It aims to remove all the barriers and inequities of the past and promote the well-being of all individuals, families, communities and society at large through accessible and appropriate mental health services. How this trickles down to community level remains the challenge.

This article describes the genesis, implementation and evaluation of a community project in a disadvantaged community. We present the development of the Jamestown Community Project (JCP) against the backdrop of several overlapping and inclusive conceptual and theoretical frameworks, namely the community psychology paradigm, program evaluation, action research and prevention. We will foreground how the project has attempted to serve the ideals of distributive equality and sufficiency, and to operationalize concepts of empowerment, participation and liberation at grassroots level.

The Context

Jamestown is a small peri-urban community of approximately 5,000 residents located on the outskirts of Stellenbosch. Set against the Hottentots Holland mountain, its tranquil panoramic and pastoral veneer, its strawberry fields, and its main street's neat appearance obscure the endemic problems, difficulties and needs that characterize rural communities long neglected in terms of the provision of health services and resources. Hidden from public view is a second community tier consisting of small pockets of informal settlements that arose when workers were displaced from surrounding farms that their families had been living on for generations. These residents are called "inkommelinge" (incomers or intruders) by the local ratepayers. Many of these residents are dependent on casual and seasonal work for a living. A third tier of the community is composed of farm workers and their families living on surrounding farms and smallholdings who use the facilities and resources in Jamestown. Many of these residents are poor, dependent on farmers, and are trapped in oppressive and exploitive socio-economic circumstances and a cycle of poverty. Approximately 60 to 70% of the learners at the primary and high schools are bussed in from farms in the district. The three tiers represent a hierarchical social class structure with tensions evident among the strata. The high level of need for psychological services at the newly-opened primary health clinic in the community in 1999 prompted the nursing manager to approach the Department of Psychology at Stellenbosch University for assistance.

The Genesis of the Project

The paucity of accessible and appropriate services in disadvantaged communities, dwindling resources and the escalation of mental health concerns, necessitate intersectoral collaboration and the application of resources in a more proactive and in both a remedial and preventive manner (Van Wyk, 2002). When the letter requesting psychological assistance landed on my desk (the first author), rather than respond to the expressed need for remedial psychological services at the primary health clinic, a series of consultation meetings were first set up with clinic staff, relevant community role-players and organizations, including the primary and high school principals, local clergy, the local governance structure and the Stellenbosch Municipality. These consultation processes served several explicit purposes: establishing formal links and personal relationships between the proposed project team and community role players, providing an informed understanding of the context of this community (its history, socio-economic conditions, psychosocial needs, and risk and resilience factors, among others), establishing the *bona fides* of the project team members, helping to identify potential partners and resources, and creating space for community input and participation from the onset. At a meeting at the clinic, set up between community role-players and the students and staff from the university, the socio-historical profile and contextual features of the Jamestown community were presented by the community leaders. The clinic nursing staff gave an overview of the presenting health concerns of residents attending the clinic, and the university role-players responded with resource and intervention options to address the emerging needs. A recurring concern was expressed for the youth of Jamestown who were becoming increasingly susceptible to alcohol and substance abuse, unplanned pregnancy, and the influence of gangs. Thus, by using key informants, a community forum, clinic statistics and other social indicators, a comprehensive needs and context analysis was obtained. At the end of this community forum meeting, the community elders formally invited the university role-players into their community.

Community Partnership

There are extant power differentials in any collaborative community project with every constituency or role-player having its own particular vested interest in the project. For example, universities are typically seen as resources of knowledge and expertise and, as a result, easily assume (and often are expected to assume) the expert, professional or leadership role in such community endeavors. Universities are also notorious for using community settings for their own agenda with little regard for, and accountability to distributive equality and sufficiency goals (Gordon and Shipman, 1988, cited in Seedat et al., 2001) essential to progressive community development. Mindful of these racial and power imbalances, the project team proposed a community partnership model to guide the development of the proposed project (Naidoo, 2000a) and to ensure that the interests, needs and accountabilities of all three parties (the community, the local municipality, and the university) would be explicitly addressed. Out of this consultative process, the following broad goals of the JCP were established: (1) The provision of counseling and psychological services at the primary health clinic to the residents of the community, workers from surrounding farms, and learners from the primary and high schools; (2) the establishment of preventive programs at the primary and high schools to deal proactively with specified needs in these settings; (3) the development of the potential of the youth in the community, by establishing relevant development and diversion programs such as leadership training, mentoring and the like; and, (4) establishing a model for community partnership.

In terms of the partnership, the community gave its endorsement and support for the project; the municipality gave permission for the project to be located at the clinic and for its resources to be used in the project; and the university undertook to provide the expertise and resources to render counseling and psychological services and other interventions (Naidoo, 2000b). The community leaders, the staff of the clinic, the principals of the secondary and primary schools, church leaders, the political and elected leadership, the Stellenbosch municipality, and other stakeholders were all consulted and were actively involved in the establishment of the project. Research underscores that the community voices and involvement are crucial to the success and sustainability of such endeavors (Petersen & Ramsay, 1993; Prilleltensky, 2001) and to more appropriate adaptations of interventions (Connell, Kubisch, Schorr & Weiss, 1995).

Levels of Intervention

The intervention conceptualization model in Figure 1, adapted from a model proposed by Brown, Pryzwansky, and Schulte (1998), provides a meaningful framework to link the goals of the project with the interventions that were developed. Mental health interventions can be con-

FIGURE 1. Conceptualising Mental Health Intervention.

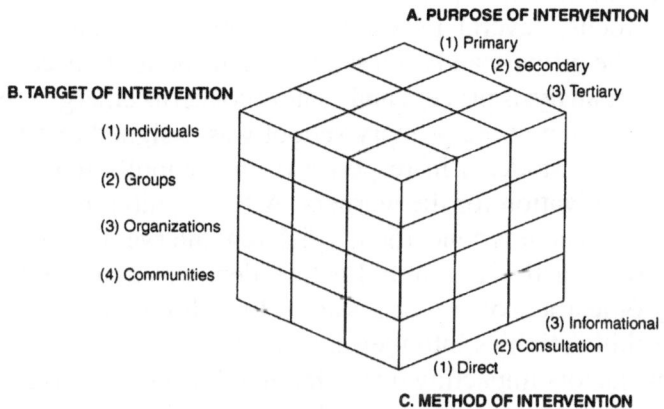

From Duane Brown, Walter B. Pryzwansky and Ann C. Schulte. *Psychological Consultation: Introduction to Theory and Pratice* (4th Edition). Published by Allyn and Bacon, Boston, MA. Copyright © 1998 by Pearson Education. Reprinted by permission of the publisher.

ceptualized on the basis of three coordinates: (a) The purpose of the intervention, (b) the target of the intervention, and (c) the method of the intervention. Caplan's (1964) typology provides the basis for differentiating the three purposes of intervening, although these should rather be seen as an intervention continuum straddling prevention, treatment, and maintenance (Scileppi et al., 2000). In practice, most interventions are multilevel, crossing over these boundaries. In community interventions, the target of intervention might include the individual but typically tends to be targeted at a group, organizational or community level. While intervention methods abound, these can be distinguished on the basis of whether the intervention involves direct interaction between the intervener and the target. Interventions can also be consultative, where the intervener works with a target group of professionals to assist with concerns they have with their tasks and responsibilities (e.g., working with teachers to brainstorm ways of handling learner discipline). Informational methods involve providing relevant information and knowledge to a target audience. These can include developing a brochure, Web site or resource center, or conducting a workshop for this specific purpose.

Primary Intervention

To broaden the conceptualization of mental health beyond the remedial-curative focus, several preventive and promotive interventions were set up at the primary and high schools, in response to needs specified in the needs analysis process and as new concerns emerged. A consultation intervention at the primary school was assigned to a team of eight postgraduate students in response to the school's request for a workshop on motivation for the learners. After an initial briefing with the principal and teachers concerned, a different intervention was negotiated as a form of action research. Each student was assigned to work with a group of learners over four sessions. In addition to incorporating relevant life skill activities into their intervention, students were asked to explore the factors impacting on the learners' level of motivation. At the end of the action research process, the consultation team compiled a joint report about their findings, then engaged with the principal and teachers concerned to share their observations and the systemic issues identified, and collaboratively developed ways of adapting the recommendations to suit the school context. The principal and the teachers then took this analysis and ideas back into their school structure and processes (Naidoo, Dunn & Van Wyk, 2001). Some of the recommendations readily implemented by the school included selecting and training class leaders in each grade who could play a role in school activities, establishing a vegetable garden for learners to take pride in their environment and their school, and training the Grade 7 learners for an active leadership role in the school. In addition, the postgraduate students continued to provide psychometric assessment sessions and conducted several life skills theme sessions with groups of learners at the school. A life skills program was also implemented at the high school with student volunteers recruited from the department's fourth year class in the facilitation role. Groups based on particular themes (such as sexuality, peer pressure, and self-esteem) identified in consultation with teachers, were set up to run weekly one-hour sessions for the duration of a semester.

A major primary prevention intervention was a youth diversion program developed in response to the community leaders' concern that the youth in the community were becoming increasingly susceptible to gang influence and to substance and alcohol abuse. In partnership with Usiko, a non-profit organization, and the high school, the program was conceptualized and operationalized based on the following corner-stones:

- The program, to run over a nine-month period, would have a strong preventive and promotive focus. (Diversion programs seek to offer youth-at-risk alternative experiences and opportunities to counteract prevailing adverse social conditions and influences. Interventions are aimed at developing the skills, potential and broadening the vision of participants).
- The participants would be young adolescent boys deemed to be "youth-at-risk."
- The program would be based on a rites of passage philosophy to offer the participants sequential guidance in their transition from boyhood to adulthood.
- The participants would undergo a wilderness excursion at the beginning and at the end of the program, as important thresholds in their rites of passage.
- A team of adult mentors from the community would be recruited and trained to guide the participants through the process.
- The participants would engage in a community project of their own choice to acknowledge their role and responsibility in their community.
- As it was being piloted, the project would be subjected to extensive evaluation.

As this intervention involved some "top-down" planning, a critical challenge involved obtaining the engagement of community members and key stakeholders. It was also difficult to reconcile stakeholder interest and community participation with funder expectations. After a community meeting to discuss the goals of the project, mentors were recruited and learners at the high school were invited to apply and motivate their personal goals for wanting to be part of the program. Teachers at the school assisted in making the final selection of 21 participants. A team of 13 men from the community was recruited as voluntary mentors using the following mechanisms: a letter to community organizations, an article about the project in the local newspaper, a radio interview, an invitation delivered to all the houses in the community, and by personal solicitation. Dual processes then unfolded with the mentors undergoing training for their role in the project. The mentees were first assessed individually (home circumstances, scholastic record, psychological profile) before they were prepared for the first wilderness experience. The nine-day wilderness experience was designed to have each participant explore his own self, life circumstances, and vision for the future through a series of guided activities. After the mentees returned from their first nine-day eventful wilderness experience, they were assigned their individual mentors. In addition to weekly meetings between mentor and mentee dyads, mentors met weekly as a group to discuss issues arising from their contact with their mentees.

Several joint activities were also convened for the mentor and mentee groups to interact. One of these activities of particular note included a visit to Robben Island where the mentees were challenged by the symbolic significance of the experience to reflect on their own situation, rise beyond the adversities that might currently imprison them (such as poverty, adverse family circumstances, and being stigmatized as farm children) and set their own vision for their future. This experience provided mentees with a valuable opportunity to reflect on their own contexts. These reflections became part of subsequent life skills sessions conducted with them at the school.

In the last month of the pilot phase, the mentees embarked on their second wilderness experience with many of the young men crossing a developmental threshold to make personal commitments regarding their lives and their vision for the future. A community graduation ceremony was held at the end of the program to celebrate their journey and their achievement. (While the evaluation of the youth project is still currently in progress, indications are that the project created a strong psychological sense of community for all involved, with many positive outcomes for the individual mentees, mentors, the school, and for the community).

Secondary Intervention

In response to the initial request, counseling and psychological services were instituted at the clinic in Jamestown in April 2000 with two postgraduate students assigned to work at the clinic two days a week. The service was targeted at individuals referred by the nursing staff and the school principals. With the increasing caseload at the primary health clinic and emerging needs at the schools, a full time counseling psychology internship was set up at the clinic for 2001. External funding was obtained for the internship after a proposal for funding submitted to the municipality had been unsuccessful. As knowledge of the internship spread, increasing referrals were made from surrounding schools, other primary health clinics, non-governmental organizations, and doctors in the Stellenbosch area (Van Wyk, 2002).

The Internship

The spectrum of services rendered by the intern at the clinic ranged from individual counseling, group therapy, psychometric and developmental assessments, consultation with nursing staff, to the presentation of workshops. Themes that emerged in therapy revolved around issues related to family relationships, difficulties with children and parenting, trauma associated with rape, child abuse, emotional abuse and violence. A predominating factor was the pernicious effects of poverty and how these impact on the lives of residents and the concomitant psychological distress. Working at the schools formed an integral part of the internship where, in addition to individual counseling, assessments, and psycho-educational services with the children, consultations were also conducted with parents and teachers. The focus was on early identification of problems—teachers are valuable community resources in facilitating this function. At the primary school, behavioral, discipline and learning problems were areas that demanded much of the intern's time. At the high school, individual psychotherapy, career counseling and life-skills workshops were the primary focus.

This range of activities reflects a necessary crossing of intervention boundaries implicit in community work. Given the isolation that typifies working in rural settings, consultation, networking and multi-disciplinary liaison were fundamental facets of this internship. At the clinic, formal consultations and informal "sharing [of] psychology" (Orford, 1992) took place with the nursing and auxiliary staff. At the schools, a consultee-centered approach was used to assist teachers with the early identification and management of behavioral and learning problems, creating an awareness of the social contexts of the learners and finding more creative solutions for class management.

Empowerment, one of the founding values of community psychology, formed an integral part of this internship. Serrano-Garcia (1984) identifies three major facets of empowerment, namely, the enhancement of personal power, creating awareness of alternative strategies to problem-solving and accessing resources in society. The consultation with the educators aimed to empower them to find alternative strategies to deal more effectively with their daily challenges and to enhance the teaching process. Consultation was also used to build capacity among the nursing staff at the primary health clinic, to create an awareness of mediating social forces and how these impact on the lives of their 'patients.' Growth in personal power through the therapy process was an important goal. For example, a few 'clients' were able to assert themselves with their employers who wanted to determine when they should attend therapy; a survivor of incest felt empowered at the conclusion of therapy to participate on a national radio program to promote awareness about incest and abuse.

The intern psychologist was also involved in the youth diversion intervention at multiple levels. Using Bronfenbrenner's (1979) levels of analysis, at a macro-level she was part of the advisory committee that planned some of the project activities, including the assessment protocol for the mentees and the project's evaluation processes. At a meso-level, she served as a consultant for the project coordinator and the school principal, ran the life skills sessions for the mentees at the school, conducted workshops with the mentors on developmental issues of adolescence and also facilitated some of the evaluation groups separately with the mentors and mentees. At a micro-level she rendered counseling and crisis intervention to several of the mentees and their family members (see Van Wyk (2002) for a detailed evaluation of this community-based internship straddling the community mental health and social-community models).

EVALUATION

Scileppi et al. (2000) define program evaluation as a type of applied research in which program characteristics, such as project goals, objectives, and costs are systematically and explicitly related to a set of values. Program evaluation is necessary and essential to arrive at meaningful formative and summative impressions that can guide project design, decision-making and accountability to stakeholders, the community, and funders. To this end, the JCP has been subjected to several independent quantitative and qualitative evaluations at different stages in the pilot phase. Monthly reports by the project coordinator, intervention reports by both groups of postgraduate students, internship evaluation reports and an annual evaluation report (Naidoo, 2000b) provide informative data about progress in the project. The Master's thesis of the second author also has provided a cogent account of the project and offers important evaluative perspectives and insightful recommendations (Van Wyk, 2002). In addition to regular focus group evaluations that were used for formative purposes (to shape subsequent direction and intermediate goals), a SWOT evaluation process was conducted at the end of the pilot phase in April 2002. This analysis became the planning basis for improving the design of the next cycle of the project. A similar evaluative process was conducted with the mentees, their teachers and parents. In addition, two independent qualitative evaluations of the project are under way as Master's research theses, one examining the project from the experience of the mentors, the other from the experience of the mentees (Naidoo, 2002).

Themes emerging from the evaluative processes indicate support from the primary health staff for the inclusion of a psychologist in their team; an expanded role for the psychologist to include curative, preventive and promotive work; the need for multi-level interventions to address community problems coupled with the importance for the psychologist to utilize different settings in the community, and the need to establish formal partnerships. While positive feedback and accolades were received for the diversion project from the mentees, mentors, parents and the school, concerns were expressed at the need to include parents and teachers more meaningfully as strategic allies and support for the project's objectives. The mentees were unanimous about the need for continued support from the mentors after graduating from the project. One of the important outcomes is that all the mentors have continued in the project for the second phase and have taken ownership of the project in their community, proposing to establish their own independent organization (Naidoo, 2002).

We have endeavored to have community voices be heard in the evaluation processes, to critically assess our progress against salient community psychology values with the aim of developing best practice protocols, and enhancing greater community participation and ownership in the next phase of the project.

CONCLUSION

Community psychology extends the agenda of psychology beyond the mainstream preoccupations of treatment and the individual. In emphasizing the need for an ecological perspective in understanding the socio-historical context of social issues, community psychology broadens the gaze to also embrace intervention goals of prevention, health promotion, development, and empowerment of individuals, groups and other social units and communities as active participants in the intervention process (Naidoo et al., 2002; Zimmerman, 2000). In the JCP, a contextual analysis of the initial presenting problem and mental health needs has led to targeting these problems with multifaceted remedial and preventive interventions and at multiple levels. We have endeavored to move away from the medical stance of pathology and deficits towards the building of competencies (Lazarus, 1988), seeking interventions that foster a psychological sense of community and empowerment, connecting individuals, organizations and the community by co-creating opportunities for residents to play an active role in gaining mastery over their lives and their community.

While more formal definitions of empowerment are beginning to emerge in the literature such as "an intentional, ongoing process centered in the local community, involving mutual respect, critical reflection, caring, and group participation, through which people lacking an equal share of valued resources gain access to, and control over these resources" (The Cornell Empowerment Group, cited in Naidoo et al., 2002), a statement by a mentor at an evaluation meeting makes this point poignantly. He said, "Niks vir ons, oor ons, sonder ons!" ("Nothing for us, about us, without us!") This sentiment has been taken to heart by the group of mentors in the pilot youth project who now stand poised to develop their own non-profit organization and will be employing three members from their own ranks to roll out the second youth project in Jamestown and another in a new community setting.

It is essential for community interventions to integrate both primary and secondary intervention objectives. However, there are a few issues with which we need to continually engage. Given the proposed integration of mental health services into the primary health care framework (Department of Health, 2002), there is concern that the existing powerful medical discourse will continue to perpetuate the pathologizing of psychological distress at the expense of understanding its social origins (Felner et al., 2000; Hook, 2002). Also, the increased workload of the primary health care practitioners could result in the neglect or displacement of mental health issues. The following statement by one such worker displays concerns about the proposed integration: "It is expected of us to be mini-doctors, now they want us to be mini-psychologists" (Van Wyk, 2002). Furthermore, much of the prevailing psychological distress dealt with in community interventions in disadvantaged communities is fundamentally symptomatic of an inequitous social system. Thus, addressing the "causes of the causes" and pursuing the value of social justice (Prilleltensky & Nelson, 1997) remain central foci that need to be targeted in community psychology.

Psychologists can play an important role in the primary and community based health care system. Local municipalities and government structures have the responsibility to establish employment opportunities for psychologists to become part of an integrated approach to primary mental health in communities.

REFERENCES

Albee, G.W. (1982). Preventing psychopathology and promoting human potential. *American Psychologist, 37*(9), 1043-1050.

Albee, G.W. (1986). Towards a just society. Lessons from observations on the primary prevention of psychopathology. *American Psychologist, 41*(8), 891-898.

Bateson, G. (1972). *Steps to an Ecology of Mind.* Chicago: University of Chicago Press.

Bronfenbrenner, U. (1979). *The ecology of human development: Experiments by nature and design.* Cambridge, Massachusetts: Harvard University Press.

Brown, D., Pryzwansky, W.B. & Schulte, A.C. (1998). *Psychological consultation: Introduction to theory and practice.* Boston, MA: Allyn and Bacon.

Caplan, G. (1964). *Principles of preventive psychiatry.* New York: Basic Books.

Connell, J.P., Kubisch, A.C., Schorr, L.B., & Weiss, C.H. (Eds.). (1995). *New approaches to evaluating community initiatives: Concepts methods, and contexts.* Washington, DC: Aspen Institute.

Department of Health. (2002). *Health Sector Strategic Framework 1999-2004.* Retrieved February 25, 2002 from the World Wide Web: *<http://196.36.153.56/doh/doc/index.html>*.

Felner, R.D., Felner, T.Y. & Silverman, M.M. (2000). Prevention in mental health and social intervention. In J. Rappaport & E. Seidman (Eds.), *Handbook of community psychology* (pp. 9-42). New York: Kluwer Academic/Plenum Publishers.

Freeman, M. (1990). The challenges facing mental health care in South Africa. In M. Freeman (Ed.), *Mental health care for a new South African and rural community mental health care* (pp. 3-11). Johannesburg: Centre for the Study of Health Policy, University of the Witwatersrand.

Hook, D. (2002). Psychotherapy, discourse and the production of psychopathology. In D. Hook & G. Eagle (Eds.), *Psychopathology and social prejudice* (pp. 20-54). Cape Town: University of Cape Town Press.

Lazarus, S. (1988). *The role of the psychologist in South African society: In search of an appropriate community psychology.* Unpublished doctoral dissertation, University of Cape Town.

Naidoo, A. (2000a). *Community psychology: Constructing community, reconstructing psychology.* Inaugural Lecture. University of Stellenbosch: University of Stellenbosch Press.

Naidoo, A.V. (2000b). *The Jamestown Community Project: Annual Report 2002.* Department of Psychology, University of Stellenbosch.

Naidoo. A.V. (2002). *The Jamestown Community Project: Evaluation Report 2000-2002*. Department of Psychology, University of Stellenbosch.

Naidoo, A.V., Dunn, M. & Van Wyk, S. (2001, August). Taking the class into the community: The application of a community consultation intervention as part of a Master's course in counseling psychology. Paper presented at PsySSA National Conference.

Naidoo, A.V., Shabalala, N. & Bawa, U. (In press). Community psychology. In L. Nicholas (Ed.), *Psychology: An introduction*. Cape Town: Van Schaik Publishers.

Orford, J. (1992). *Community psychology: Theory and practice*. Chichester: John Wiley & Sons.

Petersen, I. & Ramsay, S. (1993). Mental health and development in a shack settlement: The case of Bhambayi. *Psychology in Society, 17*, 35-50.

Pillay, Y. & Petersen, I. (1996). Current practice patterns of clinical and counseling psychologists and their attitudes to transforming mental health policies. *South African Journal of Psychology, 26*(2), 76-80.

Prilleltensky, I. & Nelson, G. (1997). Community psychology: Reclaiming social justice. In D. Fox & I. Prilleltensky (Eds.), *Critical psychology: An Introduction* (pp. 166-184). London: Sage Publications.

Prilleltensky, I. (2001). Value-based praxis in community psychology: Moving toward social justice and social action. *American Journal of Community Psychology, 29*(5), 747-778.

Scileppi, J.A., Teed, E.L. & Torres, R.D. (2000). *Community Psychology: A common sense approach to mental health*. New Jersey: Prentice-Hall.

Seedat, M., Duncan, N. & Lazarus, S. (2001). Community psychology: Theory, method and practice. In M. Seedat, N. Duncan & S. Lazarus (Eds.), *Community psychology: Theory, method and practice* (pp. 3-14). Cape Town: Oxford University Press.

Serrano-Garcia, I. (1984). The illusion of empowerment: Community development within a colonial context. In J. Rappaport, C.I.A. Swift & R. Hess (Eds.), *Studies in empowerment: Steps towards understanding action*. New York: Hawthorn.

Van Wyk, S.B. (2002). *Locating a counseling internship within a community setting*. Unpublished masters thesis, University of Stellenbosch.

World Health Organization. (2001). *The world health report 2001. Mental health: New understanding, new hope*. Retrieved February 02, 2002 from the World Wide Web: <*http://ww.who.int/whr/2001*>.

Zimmerman, M. (2000). Empowerment theory: Psychological, organizational and community levels of analysis. In J. Rappaport & E. Seidman (Eds.), *Handbook of community psychology* (pp. 43-63). New York: Kluwer Academic/Plenum Publishers.

Building Health Promoting
and Inclusive Schools in South Africa:
Community-Based Prevention in Action

Bridget Johnson
Sandy Lazarus

University of the Western Cape

SUMMARY. This paper focuses on the school as a setting for community-based prevention of factors that place learners at risk such as poverty, violence, substance abuse, learning difficulties and HIV/AIDS. It examines the development of school-based structures aimed at addressing these issues. The health promoting and inclusive schools approaches are explored as strategies to address these and other barriers to learning.

Bridget Johnson is a registered psychologist and lecturer/researcher in the Faculty of Education at the University of the Western Cape. Her main area of expertise is in educational psychology, with a particular focus on mental health promotion. Other areas of interest include health-promoting schools, HIV/AIDS and life skills education.

Sandy Lazarus is a registered psychologist and is professor and deputy dean of the Faculty of Education at the University of the Western Cape. Her main area of expertise is in community psychology, with a particular focus on the education setting in South Africa. She is extensively involved in national policy developments and restructuring related to education support services and inclusive education.

Address correspondence to: Bridget Johnson or Sandy Lazarus, Faculty of Education, University of the Western Cape, Private Bag X17, Bellville 7535, Cape Town, South Africa (E-mail: bjohnson@uwc.ac.za) (B. Johnson), (slazarus@uwc.ac.za) (S. Lazarus).

[Haworth co-indexing entry note]: "Building Health Promoting and Inclusive Schools in South Africa: Community-Based Prevention in Action." Johnson, Bridget, and Sandy Lazarus. Co-published simultaneously in *Journal of Prevention & Intervention in the Community* (The Haworth Press, Inc.) Vol. 25, No. 1, 2003, pp. 81-97; and: *Prevention and Intervention Practice in Post-Apartheid South Africa* (ed: Vijé Franchi; cons. ed: Norman Duncan) The Haworth Press, Inc., 2003, pp. 81-97.

Reference is made to innovative practice at a school in a disadvantaged community outside of Cape Town. The case study reveals how school-based teams could be utilized to mobilize school communities in generating solutions to the difficulties that they encounter. *[Article copies available for a fee from The Haworth Document Delivery Service: 1-800-HAWORTH. E-mail address: <docdelivery@haworthpress.com> Website: <http://www.HaworthPress. com> © 2003 by The Haworth Press, Inc. All rights reserved.]*

KEYWORDS. Health promoting schools, inclusive education, youth-at-risk

INTRODUCTION

Community psychology is well known for its pioneering efforts in ensuring the development of a relevant psychology for all people and for the poor and marginalized in particular. These efforts have led to explorations in the fields of education, health, welfare and public health in search of approaches and methods of practice to contribute to the overall well-being of individuals and communities. A few distinguishing features of these efforts include a focus on groups of individuals or whole communities as opposed to individuals; on prevention of problems as opposed to treatment; on empowering communities as opposed to providing solutions for them; and on working towards social change and intervening at various levels of the social system. These developments are in line with the growing interest in the field of health promotion which endorses similar principles and commitments. This endorsement includes a commitment to community-based prevention of factors that place youth at risk. This article therefore examines health promotion and inclusive education as strategies for pursuing community-based prevention of the factors that place learners at risk. These factors are explored within the context of addressing barriers to learning. The aim is to promote effective teaching and learning. As a reference point, it refers to a specific case study of a health promoting school and utilizes the lessons from the case study to inform the development of comprehensive school-based teams to meet the health and educational needs of the school community. The case study raises pertinent issues around empowerment and mobilizing communities towards generating solutions to the problems that they encounter.

Community-Based Prevention and Health Promotion

There is a growing interest in the link between community psychology and public health. This is due to the emphasis on disease prevention and the promotion of individual and social well-being within the field of public health. Public health interventions also draw upon the resources of multiple disciplines (e.g., Psychology, Anthropology, Medicine) and many different social sectors (professionals, church groups, community residents) (Butchart & Kruger, 2001). In the South African context this is particularly relevant as we aim to facilitate the process of social change and improve the well-being of all South Africans (Pretorius-Heuchert & Ahmed, 2001). With the scarce resources available for social change and community development, the pooling of human resources through intersectoral collaboration remains the most cost-effective way of affecting change (Lazarus, Moolla & Reddy, 1996). This calls for a focus on strategies and frameworks, such as the area of health promotion, that endorse these principles. Health promotion is an empowering framework that believes in providing individuals with the necessary skills to make informed decisions regarding their well-being. It recognizes the impact of external social and political influences on behavior. It therefore includes educational, political, economic, environmental and medical strategies designed to reduce disease and promote health (Reddy and Williams, 1996).

Schools as Contexts for Prevention

One of the basic features of health promotion and prevention work is understanding the role of the social setting in addition to the qualities of the person in determining behavior. According to the World Health Organization (WHO) (2000), the school is a setting where education and health programmes can have their greatest impact because they influence students at such important stages in their lives–childhood and adolescence. The implications for schools have been the broadening of approaches from the curriculum to the whole school environment and to parents and the wider community (Denman, 1998). These developments have, in turn, led to the development of health promoting schools (Downie, Tannahill & Tannahill, 1996). The health promoting schools concept strives to build health into all aspects of life at school and in the community. Health is defined as overall well-being and includes physical, social, psychological, spiritual and environmental health (Department of Health, 2000). According to the WHO (1996), the six key features of a health promoting school are that it:

- engages health and education officials, teachers and their representative organizations, students, parents, and community leaders in efforts to promote health;
- strives to provide a safe, healthy environment;
- provides skills-based health education;
- provides access to health services;
- implements health-promoting policies and practices;
- strives to improve the health of the community.

The driving force behind the development of health promoting schools is the belief that, in every community and country, children are the most important natural resource, and must be at the heart of 'development'; and that their well-being, capabilities, knowledge and energy will determine the future of villages, cities and nations around the world (WHO, 2000, p. 1).

Community-Based Prevention, Health Promoting Schools and Inclusive Education in South Africa

South Africa has adopted and commenced with implementing the health promoting schools concept in an attempt to address the historical imbalances and its consequences (Swart & Reddy, 1999). Previously, educational and health services operated in a largely fragmented manner. Access to appropriate services was limited to certain populations based on race and class. This situation placed the youth at large, and those in disadvantaged populations in particular, at risk as a result of factors such as poverty, violence, substance abuse, learning difficulties and HIV/AIDS. The recognition of the school as a key setting for intervention has led to a focus on the development of health promoting schools as a means of addressing many of the inadequacies and inequalities of existing health and education support services.

In 1994, the first health promoting schools workshop was held in Cape Town. Here representatives from various governmental sectors, education institutions and non-governmental organizations endorsed the health promoting schools concept and committed to supporting the development of health promoting schools in South Africa. It is significant that this was the first year of our new democracy when all sectors were committed to democratic principles and practice. At that time, it was important to find ways to address the inequalities of the past and to work towards unified, collaborative systems that would benefit all South Africans.

In 1995, The Reference Group for Health Promoting Schools, a voluntary multi-disciplinary network aimed at providing support for the development of health promoting schools in the Western Cape, was formed (Department of Health, 1997). What was significant about this body was the fact that it comprised individuals from the education, health, and welfare sectors, as well as non-governmental organizations who freely volunteered their time and services. It was established out of a commitment to improve the educational and health status of the children in the Western Cape. Its mandate is to provide guidance and human resources to schools who wish to develop into health promoting schools.

The first National Conference on Health Promoting Schools was held at the University of the Western Cape in 1996. At the conference, the need to transform school health and education support services was emphasized. There was a call for a more holistic, comprehensive and integrated approach to health-promotive services and programmes. This included a call for services to be more accessible and appropriate to the needs of the people (Lazarus & Reddy, 1996). The conference reaffirmed the commitment of all sectors of government to the development of health promoting schools.

In November 1997, a National Health Promoting Schools Workshop was held where it was agreed that the planning of future activities around health promoting schools should be located within local, provincial and national frameworks (Swart & Reddy, 1999). This workshop acknowledged the good work that was being done in terms of voluntary activities in developing health promoting schools. It also argued for the integration of health promoting schools activities into existing government structures and frameworks to strengthen these voluntary initiatives.

In October 2000, a draft of national guidelines for the development of health promoting schools/sites in South Africa was developed (Department of Health, 2000). What is apparent in the Guidelines is the holistic, comprehensive, cost-effective and community-oriented approach to addressing the inequalities of the past in South Africa.

The key principles outlined in the Guidelines are congruent with recent policy on inclusive education in South Africa (Department of Education, 1997, 2001). The National Commission on Special Education Needs and Training (NCSNET) and the National Committee for Education Support Services (NCESS) were established to investigate and make recommendations on all aspects of 'special needs and support services' in education and training in South Africa. The NCESS/NCSNET Report (Department of Education, 1997) highlights the fact that the previous system was not responsive to the majority of learners in South Africa. The Report recommends a shift away from a predominantly individualistic approach (seeing the individual as the one with the problem and who needs to be changed) to a systemic approach to understanding and responding to learner difficulties and disabilities. It argues that the system must be transformed to accommodate individual differences among learners. The Report proposes that the separate systems of education which presently exist ('special' and 'ordinary') need to be integrated to provide one system that is able to recognize and respond to the diverse needs of the learner population. These proposals are an attempt to assist schools to accommodate all learners. In the past, South African schools would refer 'learners with special needs' in terms of educational, physical or emotional needs to special schools. This would only benefit advantaged groups, and disadvantaged groups would not have access to these services. Often learners would have to drop out of school as the ordinary schools were not equipped to assist them. The new proposals allow all children, irrespective of their needs, to have access to education. They also make provisions for the training and development of teachers to assist learners who may require extra assistance.

The Report recommends that all centers of learning should be welcoming to all learners and other members of the teaching and learning community. The Report further recommends that all aspects of the 'health promoting school' strategy be adopted at center of learning level. This is to ensure the development of healthy school policies, supportive learning environments, strong community links, personal skills development and the provision of appropriate education support services. Lastly, it advocates the development of site-based teams to address the needs of learners, teachers and parents at local schools.

The recent White Paper 6 on building an inclusive education and training system in South Africa (Department of Education, 2001) endorses the above principles. This indicates the infusion of democratic and holistic principles into the policy documents of the government and the commitment of the government towards a quality education for all South Africans. The Paper prescribes the development of a four-tier support system aimed at assisting schools to become inclusive and supportive. It is designed to assist schools to accommodate learners with diverse learning needs which include physical, emotional, social or learning needs. The four-tier system includes appropriate competencies to provide the necessary framework for support at the national level; appropriate competencies at the provincial level; district support; and institution-based support teams.

The need for school-based assistance for learners and teachers has led to the establishment of institution-based support teams (called Teacher Support Teams (TSTs) in the Western Cape province) in many schools in South Africa. Traditional forms of TSTs have tended to focus on learning difficulties as an area of intervention, assisting teachers with the management of 'learners with special needs' as they were referred to. The process now focuses on addressing learning and teaching challenges at the school rather than referring to outside agencies. As a result of a lack of resources, there are not enough facilities and specialist services available to meet the needs of all learners. Teachers are now assisted in dealing with the problems themselves. Referrals are limited to cases that cannot be managed by the school-based team. More recently, more preventative, systemic approaches are also being developed. These include identifying all factors that contribute to the learning difficulty. Intervention strategies are then targeted at multiple levels of the system concerned, such as the home or the school environment. TSTs can be useful in providing school-based problem-based services for learners and teachers who experience barriers to teaching and learning, and can be extended to include systemic and health promoting interventions.

A CASE STUDY TO REFLECT THE RELATIONSHIP BETWEEN COMMUNITY-BASED PREVENTION, HEALTH PROMOTING SCHOOLS AND INCLUSIVE EDUCATION IN SOUTH AFRICA

A model of school-based support developed locally at a primary school in a disadvantaged area on the outskirts of Cape Town demonstrates how the health promoting school concept provides a strategy to address a range of difficulties experienced not only by learners but by teachers as well. This initiative constitutes a case study that was examined in 1996 and 1997 in terms of the development of sustainable school-based structures for addressing issues such as poverty, violence, substance abuse, learning difficulties and HIV/AIDS (Johnson, 1997).

The case study involves a primary school situated in a semi-rural town about fifty kilometers outside of Cape Town. The town is indicative of the evils of Apartheid. It was designed for so-called coloured people. They were promised housing and employment for moving to an area that lacked access to resources and that was very far away from the city center. The industries did not succeed as had been promised and the town is now faced with mass unemployment, crime, teen prostitution, substance abuse and gangsterism. Despite this grave situation, the community is committed to protecting the children and ensuring a better future for them. The development of schools into health promoting institutions is seen as a means of achieving this ideal (Flisher, Cloete, Johnson, Wigton, Adams & Joshua, 2000).

A summary of the research findings of the case study is presented according to the aims of the project, namely: (1) The initiation, development and operation of the TST, (2) the TST as a strategy for providing education support services, and, (3) the team as the nucleus of the Health Promoting School (Johnson, 1997). This paper focuses on the findings and lessons derived and not on the case study research report as such. Thus, the details of the methodology are not included.

The Initiation, Development and Operation of the TST

A governmental school health team introduced the concept of a health promoting school to the principal. The staff adapted the concept to suit the needs of their school. As the whole, staff endorsed the concept and everyone worked towards the common goal of developing a health promoting school. In the process, a collaborative team approach was developed whereby staff members served on various groups in an attempt to meet the needs of the school. The eight groups that developed addressed various aspects that are important to development and growth (see Table 1).

The school health nurse played a vital role in the maintenance of the project. She was available for assistance and motivation. She liaised with the relevant role-players and team coordinators for the provision of needed services to the school. The coordinator of the project liaised with the principal directly, keeping him informed of the progress and activities of the groups. The principal played an active role in motivating and encouraging teachers and finding solutions to difficulties encountered. He had a strong relationship with the parents and the greater community and was therefore able to gain assistance for the school: financial or otherwise. The fact that the principal and staff found a way to incorporate the activities of the project into the curriculum contributed

TABLE 1. The Eight Groups of the Health Promotion Project

Functional Group	Goals	Projects
Road safety, first aid and personal hygiene	To train teachers to train students, who would train other students. To ensure a better community.	Seminars for teachers on road safety and first aid. Teachers to attend to the personal hygiene of students on a daily basis.
Teenage club	To prepare students for the adult world. To ensure that students enter the adult world with self-confidence and responsibility.	Invited speakers to address topics such as child abuse, teenage pregnancies, personal safety, and various career choices. AIDS and TB drama for students in Grades 6 and 7.
Drug abuse	To make students aware of the dangers of drugs.To help students handle peer pressure. To make students aware of their rights as children.	Teachers attended courses where they were taught to identify various problems. There were presentations by the Child Protection Unit and South African Police Services and videos dealing with peer pressure and drugs.
After-care programme	To develop an after-care programme that is interesting, fun, recreational, stimulates cultural interest, contributes to the well-being of the community, and stimulates interest on the part of the students in community events.	(This programme did not take place because of an overload of programmes occurring after school, minimal parent and community interest, a shortage of accommodation, and a lack of funds.)
Remedial group	To assist students with learning difficulties in Afrikaans, English and Mathematics.	Provision of assistance by senior students to junior students, all junior primary teachers, and some senior primary teachers.
Youth preparedness	To create outdoor educational situations such as camps and tours.	There were speakers from 'The Fairest Cape,' excursions to Koeberg and Rondevlei Nature Reserves, a camp at Cape Point and the formation of a nature club.
Nutrition project	To be self-sustainable. To improve upon the existing feeding project. To encourage initiative. To facilitate better relationships between students. To improve communication between staff, students and parents.	Diet and lifestyle classes for students, teachers and parents. Initiation and maintenance of a vegetable garden to supplement the nutrition scheme. Growth monitoring of Grade 1 students. Dietary supplementation for athletes.
Teacher support group	To acquire healthy eating habits. To start an exercise programme. To monitor weight and blood pressure. To improve self-image. To deal more appropriately with conflict and depression.	A 'Walk it off' programme. Aerobics classes. Training in weight and blood pressure measurement. Training in behavior modification. Workshop on counseling skills.

significantly to the interest and motivation of the teachers. The incorporation of the project into the curriculum also addressed the fear of teachers regarding extra work. They were already struggling to cope and could not bear the thought of extra work. There was also a very good relationship between staff members that facilitated the process, although many interviewed argued that the relationships between staff members greatly improved as a result of the project. Staff members were committed to making the project work. Parents and learners understood the project and saw the relationship between learners and between staff and learners improving. They saw that the learners were more confident and independent. The health promotion project resulted in the school operating in a holistic manner in addressing the needs of the learners. By means of the projects, the learners were encouraged to pursue the development of their physical, psychological, social and educational potential. Their self-esteem was particularly promoted. Learners were challenged by the wide range of activities related to the projects. Positive relationships amongst all members of the school community were promoted. The development of a health-promoting environment was attempted through the establishment of the vegetable garden and the animal enclosure. Learners, teachers and parents became involved in taking responsibility for their health.

The TST as a Strategy for Providing Education Support Services

The project overcame many of the difficulties facing schools at that point in time. For example, the issue of a lack of resources was being attended to by reaching out to the parents and the greater community. Various governmental and non-governmental education support services were being accessed. Teachers were trained to deal with a wide range of problems experienced by learners. Teachers were gaining new skills and as a result were more enthusiastic about their work. Every staff member was involved in the project and as a result it was not a heavy burden on any particular member or group of teachers. The project was carefully managed and was incorporated into school management structures. This facilitated effective organization and management. Education support service personnel were involved in the project in terms of support and skills development. Historically fragmented and inaccessible services were maximally utilized through group projects with service providers becoming involved in teacher training and consultation.

The Team as the Nucleus of the Health Promoting School

The coordinating team comprised the leaders of the various groups addressing issues related to health and education. The group leaders acted as a form of TST. They met quarterly to assess the progress of the groups and to report on successes and failures. This meeting occurred with a multi-disciplinary team of service providers from within the area and surrounding areas. At these meetings ideas were generated and assistance was obtained for the groups. The team, as a coordinating body, coordinated all the activities related to developing the school into a health promoting school. The team was therefore the structure that formed the core of the health promoting school.

In short, this approach presented by the case study addresses the problem of a lack of resources, especially in terms of specialist services. It also looks at the concept of prevention and the need to lay the groundwork for a healthier society in the future. The teachers in the case study have managed to do all of this within the context of current constraints in education. These include issues such as retrenchments, increased workload, minimal resources and an atmosphere of despondency. Through their own initiatives, with the assistance of the school health team, they found a way to address the needs of their school in a cost-effective, creative manner.

KEY ISSUES AND CHALLENGES IN UTILIZING THE HEALTH PROMOTING SCHOOLS AND INCLUSIVE EDUCATION FRAMEWORKS TO PROMOTE COMMUNITY-BASED PREVENTION OF RISK BEHAVIORS AMONGST THE YOUTH

Bearing in mind the limitations, the following key lessons based on the case study could be useful in informing school-based interventions aimed at meeting the needs of impoverished communities.

Promoting the Vision of Well-Being for All Through Health Promoting Schools

It seems that an important first step in any school-based intervention is the ability to convince key role-players of the value and importance of the proposed intervention. Within the school setting this would be the principal and other senior members of staff. Once 'buy-in' at this level has been achieved, it is easier to convince the school community to attempt to do things differently. The key role-players have to be respected by the school community, however.

Mobilizing School Communities Towards the Attainment of a Common Goal

It seems that once a common goal has been identified, it is easier for members of the school community to work together to achieve this goal. The common goal could be the development of the school into a health promoting school or it could be the elimination of a particular problem such as violence, substance abuse, teenage pregnancy or HIV/AIDS.

Encouraging School Communities to Take the Initiative

It is important to encourage the school community to take the initiative in determining how they will address the challenges facing them. They need to decide what form of intervention would work best for them in the context of specific needs and resources in each school. They need the opportunity to express and test their own ideas.

Developing Structures to Sustain the Intervention

It seems that the development of structures (see Figure 1) is of paramount importance in operationalizing, managing, and maintaining theoretical constructs. Within the structures goals are set and teams are able to work towards achieving their goals. They are then able to evaluate their progress and improve their practice. The development of structures serves as an important strategy for realizing a common vision or goal.

Providing the Necessary Support and Motivation

Constant support and feedback seems to be an important factor in keeping role-players motivated to continue with the project. The support should preferably be from individuals in senior positions, as recognition and acknowledgement of good work is important.

Key Role-Players as Mediators and Support Providers

A key role-player linked to broader education and community support systems needs to be identified in the community to be available to the school community. This individual should be familiar with the dynamics of the community and be able to advise on the most successful way of working with that community. This person should also be an upstanding citizen and command respect from the community.

Good Leadership and Management to Maintain the Process

Good leadership and management are important for successful school-based interventions. School staff require guidance and assistance with new interventions. The principal needs to play a central and active role in leading, managing and developing the intervention.

Involving Parents and Communities

Many schools cite the lack of involvement of parents in the life of the school as a major problem. While generally parents seem to be disinterested in school activities, they are usually deeply involved in and affected by their children. Schools need to find ways to draw the parents into the development of the school for the purpose of fostering a supportive teaching and learning environment. In South Africa this is a particular challenge as the majority of parents have a history of disempowerment that needs to be addressed in creative ways.

A Holistic Approach to Meeting the Needs of the School Community

Health should be seen as not only physical health but also including mental, environmental, social and spiritual well-being. This should include the challenge of addressing diverse learning needs which would have a significant impact on well-being. Promoting the health and well-being of all members of the school community, and the children in particular, involves attending to all these aspects of health.

Overcoming the Difficulties of an Impoverished Environment

The case study highlights the possibility of overcoming difficulties in an environment that is plagued by uncertainty, change, a lack of resources, conflict and despondency. The ability to overcome these difficulties is facilitated by the channeling of collective energy in a new direction.

Developing the Skills of Teachers

Any initiative that contributes towards the development of skills has value and meaning for teachers. There is a dire need for teachers to upgrade their skills, especially with regard to dealing with the social and emotional issues that impact on the teaching and learning process.

Fostering a Sense of Empowerment

A sense of empowerment is created when teachers are able to take charge of an initiative and adapt it according to their particular needs. Teachers need to be placed in control of initiatives that will benefit them. They are the ones best able to understand and meet the needs of their students, parents and communities. Teachers also need to experience success in order to be encouraged to continue with a project. Small, reachable goals should be set at first and this should develop into larger, more challenging goals. When teachers experience success, it encourages them to succeed despite their difficult circumstances.

Addressing Curriculum Issues

It is important that new initiatives be built into the school curriculum. Teachers who are under pressure as a result of change will not accept any projects that could imply more work for them. Ways should be found to minimize the extra work of health projects and maximize the benefits of engaging in projects aimed at the well-being of the school community.

A TST Based on Health Promoting Principles

A TST based on the health promoting schools concept should be considered. The following example of a structure for a multidisciplinary TST based on a comprehensive needs assessment is proposed. This structure is based on the lessons gleaned from the case study.

In this model, the TST becomes a coordinating body, comprising group leaders. These group leaders co-ordinate various projects. The projects are managed by group members. The group members comprise the staff of the school, relevant education support service (ESS) personnel and, if appropriate and possible, could include parents and learners. Projects could be aimed at prevention and health promotion and include curative or problem-oriented interventions.

FIGURE 1. Possible Structure for a TST

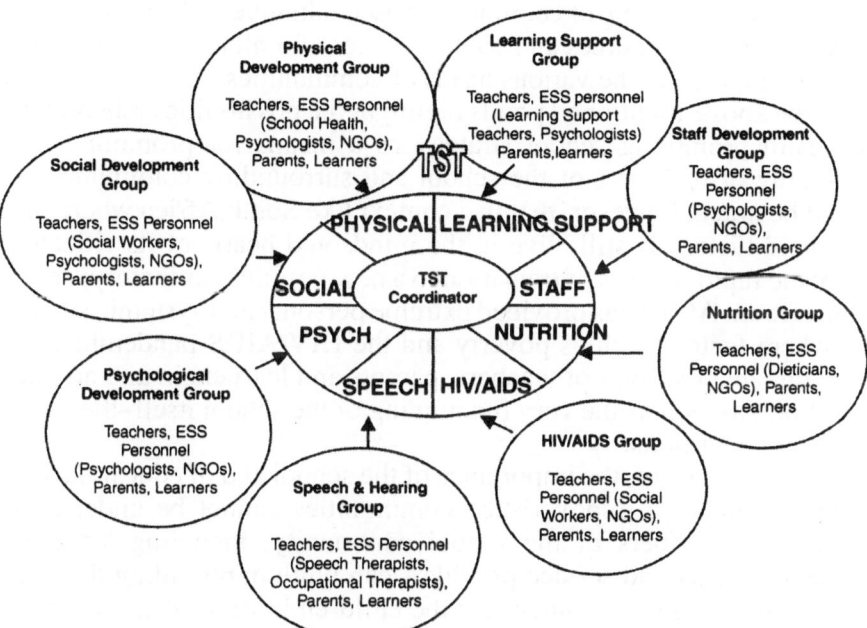

CONCLUSION

In this article the concept of community-based prevention of factors that place learners at risk has been explored within the context of a health promoting and inclusive school strategy. This article has discussed how health promotion through schools can provide a holistic and comprehensive approach to dealing with difficulties and promoting well-being. An eco-systemic view is adopted whereby difficulties which are manifested are understood not only in terms of the individual but the environment as well. As such, intervention entails the transformation of the school environment and all who form part of that environment. This strategy is congruent with community psychology which reflects an eco-systemic view of issues and includes a focus on health promotion. It allows for intervention at the individual as well as the community level. It serves to unite communities in improving their own lives as well as the lives of others. It encourages people to work together across disciplines and to utilize their strengths in meeting the needs of impoverished communities. The health promoting schools strategy is an empowering one as it encourages ownership of community-based initiatives. It allows for improved access to resources and quality services for all people. It is committed to addressing the various needs of communities.

All the above-mentioned points highlight the possibilities inherent in the health promoting school strategy as a means for promoting the well-being of members of the school and surrounding community. It should be noted, however, that in a context like South Africa where the Apartheid history is still alive in the minds and hearts of its citizens; where the rapid process of transition to a new non-discriminatory, democratic South Africa has provided extreme personal and systemic stress; and where factors such as poverty and the HIV/AIDS pandemic seriously threaten the lives of teachers, parents and learners in and around the school, as well as the very functioning of the school itself–the challenges are enormous.

Despite the above, the importance of the school and of education as a symbol of hope in impoverished communities cannot be under-estimated. All members of the school community, including learners, teachers, parents and service providers can unite in providing the best possible learning environment for the children in order that they may rise above their circumstances and realize their dreams. The health promoting schools framework, therefore, provides a useful framework for addressing the inequalities of the past in South Africa and meeting the needs of all South Africans.

REFERENCES

Butchart, A. & Kruger, J. (2001). Public health and community psychology: A case study in community-based injury prevention. In M. Seedat (Ed.), N. Duncan & S. Lazarus (Cons. Eds.), *Community Psychology. Theory, Method and Practice. South African and Other Perspectives* (pp. 215-240). Cape Town: Oxford University Press.

Denman, S. (1998). The health promoting school: Reflections on school-parent links. *Health Education, 2,* 55-58.

Department of Education (1997). *Report of the National Commission on Special Needs in Education and Training (NCSNET) and the National Committee on Education Support Services (NCESS).* Pretoria: Department of Education.

Department of Education (2001). *Education White Paper 6: Building an Inclusive Education and Training System.* Pretoria: Department of Education.

Department of Health (1997). *Health-Promoting Schools. Report on Provincial Health-Promoting Schools Networks.* Pretoria: Department of Health.

Department of Health (2000). *National Guidelines for the Development of Health Promoting Schools-Draft 4*. Pretoria: Department of Health.

Downie, R.S., Tannahill, C. & Tannahill, A. (1996). *Health Promotion: Models and Values*. Oxford: Oxford University Press.

Flisher, A., Cloete, C., Johnson, B., Wigton, A., Adams, R. & Joshua, P. (2000). Health Promoting Schools: Lessons from Avondale Primary School. In D. Donald, A. Dawes, & J. Louw (Eds.), *Addressing Childhood Adversity* (pp. 113-130). Cape Town: David Phillip Publishers.

Johnson, B. (1997). *Teacher Support Teams: A School-Based Strategy for the Provision of Education Support Services and Health Promotion*. Unpublished MPsych dissertation, University of the Western Cape.

Lazarus, S., Moolla, N. & Reddy, P. (1996, January). Intersectoral collaboration in the context of education support services in South Africa. In T. Vergnani, S. Lazarus, D. Swart, K. Bility, P. Reddy, S. James, L. Moore & O. Mobombo, *Health Promoting Schools in South Africa: Challenges for the 21st Century: Conference Proceedings* (pp. 218-233). Bellville: University of the Western Cape.

Lazarus, S. & Reddy, P. (1996). *Health Promoting Schools in South Africa: challenges for the 21st Century: Executive Summary*. Bellville: University of the Western Cape.

Pretorius-Heuchert, J.W. & Ahmed, R. (2001). Community Psychology: Past, present and future. In M. Seedat (Ed.), N. Duncan & S. Lazarus (Cons. Eds.), *Community Psychology. Theory, Method and Practice* (pp. 17-36). Cape Town: Oxford University Press.

Reddy, P. & Williams, P.M. (1996). *Defining the Concept of Health Promotion Within a School Setting*. Unpublished paper. Bellville: Medical Research Council.

Swart, D. & Reddy, P. (1999). Establishing Networks for Health Promoting Schools in South Africa. *Journal of School Health, 69* (2), 47-54.

World Health Organization (1996). *Regional Guidelines: Development of Health-Promoting Schools. A Framework for Action*. Geneva: World Health Organization.

World Health Organization (2000). *Local Action: Creating Health Promoting Schools*. Geneva: World Health Organization (Information series on school health).

Rapid Assessment Procedures:
A Participatory Action Research Approach to Field Training in Community Prevention and Intervention

Vijé Franchi

University of Lyon 2

Tanya M. Swart

University of South Africa

SUMMARY. Given the racialization of subjective, material and historical realities in South Africa, psychological training and practice in com-

Vijé Franchi (PhD) is a clinical psychologist and senior lecturer-researcher at the University of Lyon 2. Her main areas of expertise are in community and applied social psychology, with a particular focus on 'race,' youth risk behaviors, socio-politically entrenched violence, conflict resolution, intercultural processes, and identity.

Tanya M. Swart is a community counseling psychologist with a special interest in identity, violence, youth risk behaviors, and prevention in schools.

Address correspondence to: Dr. Vijé Franchi, Institute of Psychology, University of Lyon 2, Campus Porte des Alpes, 5 Av. Pierre Mendès-France, 69676 Bron Cedex (E-mail: vije.franchi@wanadoo.fr) (V. Franchi).

The authors acknowledge Winnie Kunene and the Liberty Life Foundation, and all those who participated in the 1999 Eldorado Park Community Project. In particular, the authors express their gratitude to Thabani Sibande for introducing RAP into the field training program. A special thanks to Garth Stevens, Kerry Gibson and Cheryl de la Rey for their incisive comments and reviews of earlier versions of the manuscript. The ideas and opinions expressed in this article are those of the authors.

[Haworth co-indexing entry note]: "Rapid Assessment Procedures: A Participatory Action Research Approach to Field Training in Community Prevention and Intervention." Franchi, Vijé, and Tanya M. Swart. Co-published simultaneously in *Journal of Prevention & Intervention in the Community* (The Haworth Press, Inc.) Vol. 25, No. 1, 2003, pp. 99-115; and: *Prevention and Intervention Practice in Post-Apartheid South Africa* (ed: Vijé Franchi; cons. ed: Norman Duncan) The Haworth Press, Inc., 2003, pp. 99-115.

munity raise crucial and often thorny ethical, epistemological and methodological questions. This article appraises the strengths and limitations of using Rapid Assessment Procedures (RAP) (Afonja, 1992) in the field training of postgraduate students in community-counseling psychology. Rooted in an activist participatory action research framework (Lykes, 1997), RAP provide a framework for the collective exploration of locally constructed representations of a community's needs and resources; joining the 'community' (negotiating a dialogical form of communication and a respect for the insider-outsider dialectic); working through one's 'situated otherness'; and deracializing psychological training and practice. *[Article copies available for a fee from The Haworth Document Delivery Service: 1-800-HAWORTH. E-mail address: <docdelivery@haworthpress. com>Website: <http://www.HaworthPress.com> © 2003 by The Haworth Press, Inc. All rights reserved.]*

KEYWORDS. Rapid assessment procedures, local knowledge, youth, field training, prevention in schools, participatory action research, community intervention

INTRODUCTION

South Africa's history of democracy is as recent as 1994, while its legacy of 'racially-constructed' differences, segregation, oppression and exploitation dates as far back as the colonial era.[1] Although the first democratic elections of 1994 saw the demise of apartheid as a legally entrenched system of privilege and oppression, 'racially' constructed difference continues to underpin and frame subjective, interpersonal, community, socio-economic, and organizational reality and experiences. Today, South Africans are faced with the challenges of weaving together the threads of the trauma and guilt of the past, redressing the socio-economic injustices that linger into the present, and striving for the promise of non-racial national unity, reconciliation, and upliftment in the future. In this process, groups historically constructed as belonging to different 'racial' categories may experience so-called 'intercultural misunderstanding and conflict' and tend to strengthen their ties with those who shared their social and political predicament in the past. This, together with the radically different experiences that South Africans have of the country's past and present social, political and psychological realities, may hinder the de-segregation and reconciliation of historically fragmented groups, and lead to the 'racialization' of past suffering and present positive redress measures. This predicament, the full extent of which we cannot explore further given the space constraints and the focus of this article, places considerable demands on psychology to play a key role in the transformation process. At the same time, psychology's historical links to apartheid and the 'racial' segregation of material and subjective realities in South Africa have serious and pressing implications for the training and practice of present-day psychologists.

As Duncan (2001) has pointed out, psychology as a discipline played a leading role in lending scientific legitimacy to the construction of apartheid, openly endorsed discrimination within its professional bodies, and entrenched 'racialised' inequalities in the provision of mental health care resources. Even today, in spite of corrective affirmative action measures, approximately 90% of registered psychologists in South Africa are white, and only 10% are black. Moreover, relatively few white psychologists have "[crossed] the great divide between the comfortable consultancy room and the masses" (Seedat, Cloete, Shochet, 1988). The majority of psychologists continue to deliver services to more affluent private practice and business sector clients in urban centers, and this, at the expense of what Gordon and Shipman (1988) have referred to as issues of 'distributive equality and sufficiency' in psychological practices. This refers to the meaningful contribution of psychology to the empowerment and liberation of marginalized communities. Notwithstanding the possible economic (and liberal ideological) incentives for such strategies, the unlikelihood of working across historically constructed 'racial' divides may also be related to factors such as prejudice, culture shock, experiences of 'intercultural' misunderstanding, fear and anxiety of the constructed 'Other,' guilt and remorse for having benefited from past oppression, and a denial of personal and professional responsibility in redressing the country's past and present inequalities.

A continued overemphasis on Western pseudo-universal, individual-oriented theoretical, methodological and evaluative frameworks in the curricula of professional training programs in psychology, the application of potentially discriminatory selection criteria and procedures for access into postgraduate training programs, and the unofficial tendency to match up black interns with black clients (and white interns with white clients) in some accredited training institutions, account for some of the institutional factors which may discourage or prevent black students from pursuing postgraduate training in psychology. Equally important, such practices undermine future psychologists' capacities to work across 'cultural borderlands' (Rosaldo, 1989) from a critical trans-formation perspective. A transformative perspective would include addressing the limitations of existing psychological paradigms for working in 'community' and providing relevant services to the majority of South Africans, questioning and working through the subject positions of 'insider'/'outsider' and 'other,' and challenging the 'racialization' of psychological theory and practice.

Working in the 'community'[2] in South Africa can be complicated by the fact that the very term 'community' evokes the apartheid regime's construction of geographical locations where 'racially' categorized groups, who had often been forcibly removed from their homes, were forced to live. 'Communities' so constructed exposed the majority of South Africans to differing degrees of physical, moral and material hardships, while differentially limiting their access to social, educational, and environmental resources.

Participatory action research can provide training psychologists with the tools to collectively "question dominant theoretical models for conceptualizing and responding to the effects of [political violence]" (Lykes, 1997). It provides them with a reflexive-action model for working in relevant and effective ways (Lykes & Hellstedt, 1987) across the divide of 'racialised' histories and segregated subjectivities. Born out of the need to address the empowerment and liberation of oppressed communities (Freire, 1970), participatory action research directly addresses the need to intervene at the level of community in areas ravaged by the inequalities and trauma of institutionalized, state-sponsored violence and 'racial' oppression. It proves particularly suitable as a framework for training psychologists in South Africa insofar as it provides guidelines for working from the bottom up (Rappaport, 1981), in developing trust (Straker, 1988), and co-constructing a framework for intervening in partnership with professionals and social change agents located in different sectors of a 'community.' Moreover, this approach ultimately allows the psychologist to engage in what Lykes (1997) has called "a praxis of solidarity," by teaching her or him to contest the rigid categorization of researchers' and participants' subject positions. It also endorses the importance of attempting to understand and work *with* 'cultural' groups "in their own terms" (Rosaldo, 1989), and facilitates a mutual exchange of understandings of reality and an interweaving of life experiences.

Lykes (1997) further contends that this methodology can guide the activist-researcher in exploring and constructing an understanding of a community's experiences from a position of 'situated otherness,' by helping her or him to 'stand under' the realities that she or he is grappling to connect with and make sense of. In South Africa, this approach can be used by privileged, white psychologist-activist-researchers to reflexively engage their 'situated otherness' and ethically question their 'right to speak' about the realities they observe, given their socio-historical location as beneficiaries of past and present forms of oppression and inequality.

In this article we critically appraise the applied use of Rapid Assessment Procedures (RAP) as a participatory action research framework for field training in community-counseling psychology. The article tracks the processes of learning and discovery of a group of postgraduate students who participated in a field-based training programme in 1999. It describes their applied use of RAP to identify and join partners in the 'community,' co-construct and implement 'community'-based action research, work through discourses of Othering (Riggins, 1997), and establish ways of working participatively with each other and with 'community' agents across racialized divides. Particular attention is given to the relationship between the student-researchers as outsiders and the 'community'-actors as insiders, the need to negotiate acceptance and entry into the 'community,' the tensions generated between imported and local forms of knowledges, and the use of RAP to avoid (re-)producing 'racially constructed' forms of hegemony in community prevention and intervention.

THE USE OF RAPID ASSESSMENT PROCEDURES (RAP) AS FIELD TRAINING IN PSYCHOLOGY

RAP are a relatively recent phenomenon in African social science, agricultural and health research (Afonja, 1992), and originated in response to the need to provide more relevant, multidisciplinary, and comprehensively designed research aimed at providing low-cost, effective, problem-orientated and purposeful interventions (Kachondham, 1992). They provide an holistic approach to obtaining and synthesizing relevant information about 'cultural,' 'traditional' and 'social' factors that influence individuals' perceptions, beliefs, values and cognitive representations in defining health-seeking behavior. The reported use of this methodology as a formative research tool for programme development, and as a method for collecting baseline data, monitoring health-related behaviors and evaluating interventions (Afonja, 1992), makes it particularly well suited, cost-effective and efficient for training postgraduate psychology students to participatively investigate local understandings of psychosocial problems and resources in an histori-cally underprivileged 'community.'

The training site chosen for this purpose is an apartheid-constructed, 'racially' segregated 'colored township'[3] situated 20km South West of Johannesburg. Since 1994, this urban settlement has seen the gradual integration of inhabitants and school-goers from surrounding areas (the bordering apartheid-constructed 'townships'), and the proliferation of informal settlements. Today, most of its inhabitants are working class and it has a large youth population, the majority of whom are of school-going age (Smith & Jaggan, 1996). Its poor infrastructure, in-cluding inadequate transport and public health services, and the report-edly high incidence of social problems–such as violence, crime, school drop-out, unemployment, rape, alcohol abuse, unplanned teenage preg-nancy, gang warfare, racism, and poverty (Liebowitz & Hay, 1997; Terre Blanche, 1993)–continue to bear the imprint of the unequal distri-bution of resources by the apartheid administration, and reflect current socio-economic and political struggles facing a country in transformation.

The use of RAP in this 'community' was motivated by the imperative to continue testing more action-based, participatory and contextually relevant research methodologies for the investigation of psychosocial risk and resilience issues in 'communities' in general, and amongst youth, in particular. More importantly, the initiative was developed in response to a request by local school, community and government rep-resentatives for a local university's psychology department to develop and implement a project that would address issues of violence and gangsterism among youth in the area. Such a project would provide a context in which psychology students and local change agents could continue to work collaboratively;[4] confront their fears and prejudices; experience the challenges and joys of contesting, revisiting and work-ing through socio-historically, culturally and politically learned subject positions; and, undermine the apartheid-conditioned reflexes of 'racial' discrimination and social cleavage. Equally important, it would provide training psychologists with the learning experiences necessary to be-come aware of, and work through, the 'experience of otherness' that emerges in 'intercultural' field situations, and the fear of not being able to communicate with socio-historically defined 'Others.'

RAP are based on a bottom-up response-demanding model of inter-action (Gran, 1983), that gives priority to indigenous and locally con-structed knowledges (Kachondham, 1992), and highlights the importance of co-constructing understandings of social problems with the people concerned. As such, they provide a useful framework for training students in critical 'intercultural' community psychology. The focus on involving the people concerned by the intervention in the problem identification, planning, implementation and evaluation stages–all of which form one single process towards creating change–sensitizes students to the importance of reciprocity and collaboration between the external and local agents benefiting from a social transformation program. Equally important, the recognition of the 'socio-cultural' and historical constructedness of local needs and resources encourages students to legitimate the subjective meanings that local agents attribute to life events, over and above the externally–imposed theoretical understandings that they would be tempted to bring. This increases the likelihood that the findings generated by a study will be used to develop an intervention relevant to those concerned (Montero, 1998).

RAP was considered to be, in and of itself, an awareness raising and 'intercultural' dialogue intervention. Firstly, it would provide students with a context for acquiring experiential knowledge with regard to working ethically as psychologists across racialized divides, in 'community' contexts ravaged by apartheid. Secondly, it would encourage them to face their sense of 'otherness' and question the implications of their subject position as 'dominant,' researcher, and trainee psychologist. Lastly, by focusing their attention on the needs of 'community' members and on local understandings of the causes, priorities and nature of the problems described, it would increase their likelihood of making isomorphic attributions (Brislin, Cushner, Cherrie & Yong, 1986), thereby strengthening their ties with local change agents. From a systemic perspective, the use of RAP was intended to help students negotiate a way of joining with the host community–by recognizing the different yet interconnected levels of the system, each with its own definitions of community needs and resources–and working *with*, and alongside, rather than on, or in the place of, local change agents.

THE RAPID ASSESSMENT PROCEDURES PROCESS

Trainees

Trainees included a gender-balanced and heterogeneous group of 12 postgraduate students in community psychology. Heterogeneity in terms of socio-linguistic, religious, residential, and economic backgrounds, as well as historically designated apartheid 'racial' categories, ensured the possibility of working with and through issues of racialized understandings and approaches to 'community' and psychological practice, both within the group and within the 'community' project.

Training and Preparation

Theoretical training was provided by two academic staff members. The first provided training in the RAP methodology, while the second ran a semester-long course in critical 'intercultural' psychology. RAP were presented to the students as a systematic, action-oriented approach to research, carried out in a limited period of time. They were informed that data collection procedures could include formal and informal interviews, conversations with well-informed individuals or groups, observations, participant observations, and focus group discussions (Afonja, 1992). Lastly, informants would have to be chosen on the basis of their ability to provide direct and relevant information in the limited time period required.

The critical 'intercultural' psychology course provided a theoretical framework for analyzing their experiential learning in areas related to 'intercultural' communication (social categorization, prejudice, the ideology of racism, errors of attribution, 'culture' shock, etc.), and practice (ethical considerations related to the use of emic- versus etic-type assessment, intervention and treatment approaches), as well as critical questions of self-identity, identification and the role of language in 'community' prevention and intervention. The students were supervised in working through the 'racially' constructed divides among themselves, as a basis for their later work within and with the 'community.'

Methods

As part of their RAP training, students selected three methods for exploring local representations and understandings of 'community', and local resources and needs, namely: (1) semi-structured interviews and conversations with informed community members; (2) focus group discussions; and (3) observations. The same set of open-ended questions[5] served as a guideline in both the semi-structured interviews and informal exchanges and in the focus groups. These included questions such as: How would you describe your community? What would you consider to be the strengths of your community? Are there any problems that you feel are a cause for concern within your community? In the interviews, the questions provided a combination of flexibility and guidance, allowing both the respondent and the interviewer to move the discussion in different directions (de Haas, 1997). This provided the containment needed to establish trust and confidentiality, while ensuring enough space and freedom to create and co-construct understandings of reality. The focus groups, on the other hand, included six to eight participants each, and were run by two or three facilitators (one or two student(s) and a person from the local 'community'). The facilitators alternated between recording, moderating, translating and re-directing the discussion in line with these broad questions. This method facilitated access to issues that would have proven inaccessible were it not for the dynamic interactions that a group produces (Morgan, 1988). Lastly, the observation group focused on observing, describing and exploring aspects of social life within the 'community,' as these take form and are displayed in the physical structures, daily life and activities of its inhabitants. This entailed observing events as they arose, irrespective of how dramatic or mundane, and noting both the implicit and explicit aspects of these phenomena (Newman, 1997).

Data collection was conducted in two sessions over a two-week period. On the first occasion, the field researchers were based at several sites, including a recreation center, residential areas, the local police station, a clinic, various religious institutions, and the central area where the main road and most businesses are located. On the second occasion, the teams worked in and between two local schools. The only necessary requirements for the selection of respondents were that they be in possession of local knowledge and be willing to participate in the research process.

The data were transcribed after each session and subsequently content analyzed for emergent themes. The information obtained using the different methods and for the different sub-samples of respondents was then triangulated. This refers to the cross-referencing of commonalities, differences or patterns that emerge in the use or meaning that the themes have in a particular data set or for a given group of informants. It is in this dynamic mix of similarity and difference that one may come to perceive the contours of the meaning attributed to life events and people's personal and collective experiences of them. Lastly, the findings were fed back to the respondents and other 'community members.' This restitution provided a participatory forum in which results could be verified, discussed, debated, negotiated and shared with the people concerned. Additionally, it provided a sense of closure to the research process, and a platform for future action.

Supervision

The participants' fieldwork was supervised by three second-year postgraduate students, who organized and coordinated the groups' activities and provided weekly debriefing on site. They also acted as *gatekeepers*, and were able to secure the students' access into various sites in the 'community' and the tolerance of their presence there, by virtue of their previous involvement in projects in the area and interactions with recognized community leaders.[6] Weekly supervision was also provided at the university by a qualified psychologist.

IDEAS EMERGING FROM THE RESEARCH

A total of 46 interviews, eight focus group discussions, and two observations were conducted. Focus group participants and interviewees included educators, learners, youth who had participated in previous community projects, religious leaders, police, residents, shopkeepers, youth leaders and health care professionals. The analysis of the data generated a set of 18 inter-related and articulated themes, which provide a kaleidoscope view of the respondents' perspectives of the strengths, hopes, concerns, challenges, and daily realities of people living in this neighborhood.[7] Whilst it is not within the scope of this paper to give a detailed account of the findings, a brief summary is provided below.

Local Understandings of the 'Community,' Its Risks and Resources

Overall, respondents reported a perceived lack of a sense of community, particularly in comparison with the strong sense of community evident during apartheid, when shared feelings of marginalization had united people across racially constructed divides in a joint struggle for liberation against a common oppressor. Reasons provided for the absence or fragmentation of a sense of community included the feeling that 'colored's' were a neglected population group in the new dispensation; the lack of sufficient socialization or interaction between parents and children; the escalating levels of gangsterism in the area and, from a youth perspective, the lack of prospects offered by the community.

The data collected regarding the risk factors to youth in this area corroborated some of the findings in the existing literature (e.g., Smith & Jaggan, 1995; Swart, Seedat, Ricardo & Johnson, 1999; Terre Blanche,

1993). The data indicated exceptionally high levels of unemployment; alcohol and drug abuse; urban (assault, homicide, etc.), interpersonal (spousal and child abuse), and sexual violence; gangsterism; crime; exposure to high levels of stress related to daily violence or the threat thereof; 'racial' and religious discrimination; school failure, drop-out, absenteeism, and a lack of respect for educators; poor or violent intergenerational relationships; and unplanned teenage pregnancy.

The 'community' was described by numerous respondents as being "under-resourced," especially in terms of recreational facilities and activities for children and youth. While churches offered some recreational activities, these services were seen as inadequate, resulting in a disinvested, frustrated and very bored youth population, which predisposed them to involvement in crime and substance abuse. In the absence of adequate role models and recreational outlets, youth were seen to aspire to becoming gangsters or criminals who represent the 'rags to riches' ideal, and in many instances, a welcome escape from the material and social restraints of poverty, unemployment, family strife and violence. The lack of social and psychological support structures for youth within the 'community' was also raised as a concern by youth and adults alike, as too were the inadequate medical facilities, counseling services and an understaffed police service.

Where community resources were mentioned, this was often accompanied by a certain ambivalence regarding their limitations in providing material assistance (as in the case of churches), solace in the face of diversity, or solutions to the social problems of local adults, youth and children. For instance, though religion was perceived as a source of comfort for many young people, it also sometimes led to peer rejection. Similarly, while school was seen to provide youth with increased life opportunities, and educators were often a positive influence in their lives, the sexual involvement of educators with female students was often mentioned by respondents. Peer groups and older youth provided love, guidance and a sense of belonging for younger children. However, their influence was also potentially detrimental, insofar as younger children may be exposed to drinking, drugs and criminal activities.

Experiences and Process Issues Related to RAP Field Training

In evaluating their experiences of RAP, students found that the process had afforded them a unique learning opportunity which had touched their lives deeply, allowed them to develop greater self-reflexivity, and altered their approach to psychology and working in South Africa.

They found the data collection both exciting and distressing. While the collective inquiry was useful for gathering relevant information and provided a first opportunity for practical experience in community psychology, most students felt overwhelmed by the reality portrayed in respondents' narratives. They found the process emotionally demanding, particularly when it entailed investigating dire emotional and physical life circumstances. Most students experienced extreme helplessness when faced with recording the personal experiences of sexual harassment, rape, and child abuse. They found the vivid descriptions by some participants of violent incidents in the 'community,' without shows of emotion or difficulty, shocking if not traumatic. These left them speechless, depressed, "not knowing," wanting to blame someone (but who? the past, parents, educators, the government?), seeing inadequacy in theory, in themselves and others, and not wishing to "go there again." The initial thrill and excitement of the participatory research process was dampened by the overwhelming expectations that 'community' members had for change and intervention. They were faced with working through the enormity of the hardships they encountered, while drawing strength from those aspects of the community work that they found rewarding.

Students reported finding themselves constantly having to negotiate their previously held assumptions and stereotypes with regard to the 'community,' and sociopolitical problems such as poverty, 'race,' crime and drug-taking behavior. The students' initial, preconceived understandings of the 'community' were indicative of their own historical location in South Africa, and in many ways reflected the racialization of these experiences. Some students viewed the 'community' as a 'colored' community, defined in terms of skin color and language, while others perceived it as comprised of people of 'colored' origin, who are of a lower socio-economic status or disadvantaged. Still others perceived this 'community' as enjoying a higher socio-economic status to that of 'African' people, by virtue of the fact that 'colored,' 'white' and 'Indian' people, unlike so-called 'Africans' (defined according to the 'racial' nomenclature of apartheid), had been represented in the former apartheid government's parliament. These students contended that 'Africans' had been the most severely brutalized and oppressed during apartheid, and had been economically exploited to the advantage of the other 'races,' including 'coloreds.' They perceived 'coloreds' as adopting 'racially' superior attitudes and being racist towards 'African' people. These students found it difficult to conceive of a 'coloured' 'community' as being disadvantaged, knowing the living conditions of

'African' people within their own 'communities.' They perceived an intervention in a 'coloured' 'community' as being not only irrelevant, but a perpetuation of the neglect of 'African' 'communities.' In addition to confronting their own prejudices and stereotypes, students had to negotiate those of 'community' members, as well as their position of 'outsider,' as defined by their university affiliation, language use and 'racially' ascribed identities.

At a methodological level, students criticized RAP for creating a false division between data collection methods, as they found that these methods overlapped both at a process level and in terms of the information gathered. Moreover, while the focus group discussions proved useful when working with historically marginalized people, language barriers were a problem. The participants used this opportunity to enthusiastically engage in debates, but frequently lapsed from English into Afrikaans, especially when they felt a need to be more expressive. Even students who were proficient in Afrikaans found it difficult to understand the participants' particular use of certain terms and concepts.

DISCUSSION

Overall, the RAP provided a framework which met the criteria for training psychologists outlined by Gibson, Sandenbergh, and Swartz (2001): It facilitated contained and well-structured exposure to the 'community,' capitalized on the students' existing skills while encouraging a critical transformation of their perspectives for working in 'community,' and provided structured, on-going supervision which enabled students to monitor subjective and intersubjective processes and fostered greater reflexivity. Students were able to negotiate a way of joining different groups in the 'community'; co-constructing understandings of the 'community,' youth risk behaviors, and resources; and re-defining a participatory role for themselves as researchers and for the respondents as partners. They reported having experienced the rewards of exploring, defining, feeding back and developing hypotheses about the causes of problems and the possibilities for intervention collectively, with the social agents concerned by the intervention. Moreover, they experimented ways of integrating processes of local and specialized knowledge production, finding a place for insider and outsider forms of expertise, and weaving together socio-historically and subjectively anchored and disparate viewpoints amongst themselves and across the student-'community' divide.

Finally, on-site training in a historically oppressed 'community' in South Africa provided a context for addressing the necessity to deracialize subjective and interpersonal processes and theoretical and methodological approaches in Psychology. The opportunity to be trained and work in a group comprising students from different historically defined 'racial' groups, as well as gender, class and language groups, whose subject positions embodied the historically constructed insights and blind spots that made them both differently sensitive and selectively impervious to certain 'real' and imagined social realities and needs of local partners, provided a contained space within which to work through issues which would later be encountered in the 'community.' Working in 'community' later allowed them to contest their socio-politically, historically, culturally and ideographically situated understandings and experiences of themselves and people in historically segregated and marginalized communities. Equally important, it enabled them to work through their feelings of 'otherness'–what Freud (1919b/1985) referred to as *'das unheimliche'* (a feeling of disquietening unfamiliarity)–which were intensified by the asymmetrical nature of racialized interactions and the ethnocentrism of their own initial understandings of self and other. The collective analysis of these processes through debriefing and supervision sessions allowed students to de-center the self from its narrow socio-political, historical, cultural, subjective, and gendered frames of reference. This process resulted in what Gadamer (in Taylor, 1994) calls a 'fusion of horizons,' in which the newly encountered and as yet unfamiliar frame of reference is integrated and placed alongside the framework initially used to valuate reality, thereby broadening the lexicon used to understand and compare the worth and meaning of these different systems.

Equally important, by adopting, as Lykes (1997) puts it, a position of participant observer 'standing under' the realities observed, they were able to shift their positionality and integrate the local knowledge and awareness gleaned through RAP. The focus on local understandings and knowledges helped them to challenge and shift their initial stereotypical representations of this urban settlement and its youth's identity aspirations and fears. Similarly, students who felt that the group should be working in black communities where there is 'real' need were able to work through and shift their racialized perceptions of need and resource.

For the local participants, the processes involved in co-constructing understandings with outsiders opened a possibility for threading together different histories of South Africa, finding shared experiences across 'racially constructed' divides, working through some of the daily trauma of past and present political, material, and social forms of strife and structurally entrenched violence, and reclaiming the personal and collective power and agency necessary to face these phenomena. The recognition and respect for local meanings and experiences opened up a contained space for participants to express their shared and personal anger, indignation, symbolic rejection of the 'historically privileged' outsider, and desire for change. In this process, they acquired the confidence to negotiate cautious interaction, stilting trust, and partial identification across racialized divides.

NOTES

1. See Goldin (1987), Brown and Butchart (1991) for a more detailed discussion.
2. The authors place the word community in inverted commas to signify our critical contestation of externally imposed understandings of community.
3. See Simms (1999) for a discussion of the systematic and forced removal, relocation, and segregation of South Africans within specified residential areas during apartheid.
4. At the time, a three-year Early Childhood Enrichment Project, in which psychology students had been working collaboratively with local youth in providing psychosocial education to young children, was drawing to a close.
5. Slightly different versions were prepared for use with youth and adults respectively.
6. Multiple leaders in a 'community' may be officially and unofficially recognized by different groups as capable of representing them to differing degrees in different areas.
7. These themes are not dealt with directly in this article but are explored in detail in an upcoming article currently being prepared for this purpose.

REFERENCES

Afonja, S.A. (1992). Rapid Assessment Methodologies: Application to health and nutrition programmes in Africa. In N.S. Scrimshaw & G.R. Gleason (Eds.), *Rapid Assessment Procedures* (pp. 81-94). Boston: International Nutrition Foundation for Developing Countries (INFDC).
Brislin, R.W., Cushner, K., Cherrie, C. & Yong, M. (1986). *Intercultural Interactions: A practical guide.* Beverly Hills, CA: Sage.
Brown, D. & Butchart, A. (1991). Non-fatal injuries due to interpersonal violence in Johannesburg-Soweto: Incidence, determinants and consequences. *Forensic Science International, 52,* 35-51.
de Haas, M. (1997). *Interviewing.* Durban: University of Natal.
Duncan, N. (2001). Psychologie et politique en Afrique du Sud: Quels liens? [Possible links between psychology and politics in South Africa] *Canal Psy, 50,* 10-12.
Freire, P. (1970). *Pedagogy of the oppressed.* New York: Seabury Press.

Freud, S. (1919b/1985). *L'inquiétante étrangeté et autres essais. [The familiar strangeness and other essays].* Paris: Gallimard.

Gibson, K., Sandenbergh, R. & Swartz, L. (2001). Becoming a community clinical psychologist: Integration of community and clinical practices in psychologist's training. *South African Journal of Psychology, 31*(1), 29-35.

Goldin, I. (1987). Making race: The politics and economics of coloured identity in South Africa. Cape Town: Maskew Miller Longman.

Gordon, E.W. & Shipman, S. (1988). Human diversity and pedagogy. In E.W. Gordon and Associates (Eds.), *Human diversity and pedagogy.* New Haven: Yale University.

Gran, G. (1983). *Development by people: Citizen construction of a just world.* New York: Praeger.

Kachondham, Y. (1992). Rapid rural appraisal and rapid assessment procedures: A comparison. In N.S. Scrimshaw & G.R. Gleason (Eds.), *RAP: Rapid Assessment Procedures.* Boston: INFDC.

Liebowitz, S. & Hay, W. (1997). Adolescent notions of self and community: The implications of a community-based intervention program in a South African Township: Unpublished paper.

Lykes, M.B. (1997). Activist participatory research among the Maya of Guatamala: Constructing meanings from situated knowledge. *Journal of Social Issues, 53*(4), 725-746.

Lykes, M.B. & Hellstedt, J.C. (1987). Field training in community-social psychology: A competency-based, self-directed learning model. *Journal of Community Psychology, 15*, 417-428.

Montero, M. (1998). Dialectic between active minorities and majorities: A study of social influence in the community. *Journal of Community Psychology, 26*(3), 281-289.

Morgan, D. (1988). *Focus groups as qualitative research.* Newbury Park, California: Sage Publications.

Newman, W. (1997). *Social research methods: Qualitative and quantitative approaches* (third edition). Boston: Allyn and Bacon.

Rappaport, J. (1981). In praise of paradox: A social policy of empowerment over prevention. *American Journal of Community Psychology, 9*(1), 1-21.

Riggins, S.H. (1997). The rhetoric of Othering. In S.H. Higgins (Ed.), *The language and politics of Exclusion: Others in discourse* (pp. 1-30). Thousand Oaks, CA: Sage.

Rosaldo, R. (1989). *Culture and Truth: The remaking of social analysis.* Boston: Beacon Press.

Seedat, M., Cloete, N. & Shochet, I. (1988). Community psychology: Panic or panacea. *Psychology in Society, 11*, 39-54.

Seedat, M., Duncan, N. & Lazarus, S. (2001). Community psychology: Theory, method, and practice. In M. Seedat, N. Duncan & S. Lazarus (Eds.), *Community Psychology. Theory, Method and Practice* (pp. 3-14). Cape Town: Oxford University Press.

Smith, D. & Jaggan, V. (1995). *The People's History Project: A case study in the importance of social and community identity in violence prevention.* Institute for Social and Health Sciences: Unpublished programme document.

Straker, G. (1988). The continuous traumatic stress syndrome–The single therapeutic interview. *Psychology in Society, 8*, 49-79.

Swart, L., Seedat, M., Ricardo, I., & Johnson, K. (1999). Eldorado Park High Schools Safety Promotion and Health Survey. ISHS/CPA Community Technical Report Series, No.2.

Taylor, C. (1994). The politics of recognition. In A. Guttman (Ed.), *Multiculturalism* (pp. 95-102). Princeton, NJ: Princeton University Press.

Terre Blanche, M. (1993). Putting psychology to work in the community: Focus on the Center for Peace Action (CPA), *Unisa Psychologia*, 20(1), 4-11.

Index

Accreditation, of leadership programs, 61-62
African National Congress, 38
AIDS/HIV, epidemiology, 2
American Psychological Association research guidelines, 34
Apartheid, 1-2
    psychology's support of, 101
Autonomy, 5

Block modules, 57-58

(University of) Cape Town, 49-64
Community, as racialized term, 102, 110-111
Community context, 4-5
Community development approach, as compared with public health, 16-17
Community psychology
    curative/preventive interventions, 65-80. See also Jamestown Community Project
    current status of, 3
    role of, 2-3
Context, community, 4-5
Council for Scientific and Industrial Research, 38
Cultural issues, 99-102

Developmental behavior theories, 66-67
Distributive sufficiency, 3

Empowerment, 3-4,56,94

Environmental impoverishment, 93

Firearms Control Bill, 41

Gender issues, in leadership programs, 57
Gun-Free South Africa, 39
Gun Lobby, 41

Health promoting schools, 81-97. See also Schools-based intervention
"Helping" professions, paternalism and, 4-5

Inclusive education, 81-97. See also Schools-based intervention
In Praise of Paradox (Rappaport), 4
Intercultural misunderstanding, 100-101
Interdisciplinarity, 11-29. See also Methodological pluralism

Jamestown Community Project, 65-80
    background and principles, 66-68
    community partnership, 69-70
    conclusion, 77-79
    context, 68
    evaluation, 76-77
    genesis of project, 69
    internship, 75-76
    levels of intervention, 70-71
    primary intervention, 72-74
    secondary intervention, 74-75

Leadership
   stereotyping and, 51
   trait theory of, 51
Leadership training programs, for
      women, 49-64. *See also*
      Women's leadership
      programs
Lewin's behavioral equation, 66
(University of) Lyon 2,1-9,99-115

Mental health interventions, levels of,
      70-71
Methodological pluralism, 11-29
   neighborhood-based violence
      prevention, 19-25
   public health/community
      development approach,
      15-19
   violence prevention challenges,
      13-15
Motivation, for leadership training, 56
Multilevel interventions, 65-80. *See
      also* Jamestown Community
      Project

National Commission on Special
      Education News and Training
      (South Africa),
      85-86
National Committee for Education
      Support Services (South
      Africa), 85-86
National Conference on Health
      Promoting Schools (South
      Africa), 85
Networking, women's, 59
Non-governmental organizations
      (NGOs), 13-14

Participatory action approach, 99-115.
      See also Rapid Assessment
      Procedures
   development of method, 102-103

discussion, 111-113
   ideas emerging from, 108-111
Participatory learning, 58-59
Payment, for leadership training, 55-56
Preventive initiatives, efficacy of, 67
Problem definition, politics of, 66-67
Psychological after-care, in violence
      prevention, 23
Psychology profession, in supporting
      apartheid, 101
Public health/community development
      approach, 15-19
Public health model
   appropriateness and value, 16
   four steps of, 16

Racially constructed differences,
      100-101
Rapid Assessment Procedures
   as field training, 103-105,108-111
   process of, 105-108
Reconstruction and Development
      Program (South Africa), 35
Reference Group for Health Promoting
      Schools (South Africa), 85
Research/service-delivery schism,
      14-15

Safety and Security Portfolio
      Committee, 41
Schools-based intervention, 81-97
   background and principles, 82-83
   in community mobilization, 92
   conclusion, 95-96
   curriculum issues, 94
   empowerment and, 94
   environmental impoverishment and,
      93
   health promotion and community,
      83
   holistic approach in, 93
   inclusive education and, 84-87
   initiation and sustainment, 92

key role-players, 93
leadership and management, 93
parent/community involvement, 93
schools as prevention context,
83-84
support and motivation for, 92
teacher-skills development, 94
Teacher Support Teams, 87-91,
94-95
as visionary influence, 91-92
WHO guidelines for, 84
Service delivery, 13-15
Service delivery/research schism,
14-15
Social class, 68
Socioeconomic status, 2
(University of) South Africa, 1-9,
11-29,31-47,49-64,99-115
South African Department of Arts,
Culture, Science and
Technology (DACST), 35
South African health policy, 34-35
South African National Injury
Mortality Surveillance
System (NIMSS)
background, 32-34
conclusion, 45
content factors in usage, 33,39,42
contextual factors in usage, 33,38,
41-42
data initiatives and methodology,
35-37
findings, 38-45
health policy context, 34-35
process factors in usage, 33,39-41,
42
purpose and aims, 34
social actors' influences, 33,41,44
summary findings, 44-45
Three Neighborhood Safety
Promotion Study, 37-45
usage, 37-38
Southern Metropolitan Local
Council, 37

Standardization, of leadership
programs, 61-62
(University of) Stellenbosch, 65-80

Teacher-skills development, 94
Teacher Support Teams, 94-95
case study, 87-91
in education support, 90
establishment of, 87,88-90
as nucleus of health promotion, 91
Theoretical diversity, 11-29. *See also*
Methodological pluralism
Three Neighborhood Safety Promotion
Study, 36-45
Trait theory of leadership, 51

Uniqueness, of communities and
solutions, 5
University of Cape Town, 49-64
University of Lyon 2, 1-9,99-115
University of South Africa, 1-9,
11-29,49-64,99-115
University of Stellenbosch, 65-80
University of Western Cape, 81-97

Violence, macro-level appoaches,
18-19
Violence prevention, 11-29
challenges in South Africa, 13-15
conclusion, 25-26
epidemiological data in, 31-47. *See
also* South African National
Injury Mortality Surveillance
System (NIMSS)
lack of research, 14-15
neighborhood-based initiative,
19-25
public health/community
development approach, 15-19
Violence prevention matrix
home-based after-care, 24
home visitation program, 22-23

principles, 17-19
psychological after-care, 23
schools-based initiative, 22
social support intervention, 23
Step 1: qualitative/quantitative data
    collection,, 19-20
Step 2: analytical processes, 20-21
Step 3: development of initiatives,
    21-24
Step 4: evaluation, 24-25

(University of) Western Cape, 81-97
White Paper 6,86-87
Women's leadership programs, 49-64
    accreditation, 61-62
    block modules, 57-58
    conclusion, 62
    creative evaluation approaches, 59
    data analysis, 54
    data collection, 53-54
    defining leadership, 57
    empowerment, 56

findings and discussion, 54-62
gender issues, 57
motivation for training, 56
networking, 59
participatory learning, 58-59
payment for training, 55-56
sample profile, 54
standardization, 61-62
study follow-up and site visits, 60
target groups and context, 55
techniques and strategies, 57-62
theoretical issues, 51-53
women-only *vs.* mixed gender
    training, 60-61
World Health Assembly (WHA), 35
World Health Organization (WHO),
    35,67-68,83-84

Youth-at-risk, 81-97. *See also*
    Schools-based intervention
Youth field training, 99-115. *See also*
    Rapid Assessment
    Procedures